A CAREGIVER'S Survival GUIDE

How to Stay Healthy *When Your Loved One Is Sick*

Kay Marshall Strom

IVP Books

An imprint of InterVarsity Press
Downers Grove, Illinois

InterVarsity Press
P.O. Box 1400, Downers Grove, IL 60515-1426
World Wide Web: www.ivpress.com
E-mail: email@ivpress.com

InterVarsity Press® is the book-publishing division of InterVarsity Christian Fellowship/USA®, a
movement of students and faculty active on campus at hundreds of universities, colleges and
schools of nursing in the United States of America, and a member movement of the International
Fellowship of Evangelical Students. For information about local and regional activities, write
Public Relations Dept., InterVarsity Christian Fellowship/USA, 6400 Schroeder Rd., P.O. Box 7895,
Madison, WI 53707-7895, or visit the IVCF website at <www.intervarsity.org>.

All Scripture quotations, unless otherwise indicated, are taken from the Holy Bible, New
International Version®. NIV®. Copyright ©1973, 1978, 1984 by International Bible Society. Used
by permission of Zondervan Publishing House. All rights reserved.

Cover photograph: John Henley/The Stock Market

ISBN 978-0-8308-2230-0

Printed in the United States of America ∞

Library of Congress Cataloging-in-Publication Data

Strom, Kay Marshall, 1943-
   A caregiver's survival guide : how to stay healthy when your loved one is sick / Kay
Marshall Strom.
       p. cm.
   Includes bibliographical references.
   ISBN 0-8308-2230-5 (pbk. : alk. paper)
   1. Caregivers—Religious life. 2. Caring—Religious aspects—Christianity. I. Title.

BV4910.9 .S78 2000
259'.4—dc21
                                                                                    00-039589

| P | 23 | 22 | 21 | 20 | 19 | 18 | 17 | 16 | 15 | 14 | 13 | 12 | 11 | 10 | 9 |
| Y | 24 | 23 | 22 | 21 | 20 | 19 | 18 | 17 | 16 | 15 | 14 | 13 | 12 | 11 | |

I lovingly dedicate this book to my family,
who never failed to give me their loving support.
A special thanks to my daughter and son-in-law
Lisa and Arie Ringnalda
and to my son
Eric Strom.
I include in this dedication Dan Kline,
who throughout my journey was a good and caring friend
and is now my good and caring husband.

Contents

Before You Begin

Honesty is always the best policy, but especially when you're among a crowd of ladies in a restroom during a break at a women's conference. One well-dressed woman, putting on lipstick, said, "Oh, Joni, you always look so together, so happy in your wheelchair. I wish I had your joy!" Several around her nodded. "How *do* you do it?" she said as she capped her lipstick.

I glanced at the girls around me, all of them sharply dressed. I knew the break would soon be over. How could I sum up in a sound bite what has taken three decades of quadriplegia to learn?

"I *don't* do it," I said. That raised eyebrows. "In fact, may I tell you honestly how I woke up this morning?" Several women leaned against the counter to listen.

"I thought, *Oh Lord, I'm about to get a bed bath, get dressed and be lifted into my wheelchair. My hair will get brushed, and so will my teeth. I've been through this routine countless times, and I don't have strength to face it this morning. I have no resources. I don't have a smile to take into the day, but you do. May I borrow yours? I urgently need you, God. I require you desperately.* Only then am I able to smile. But it's not my smile, it's God's. Whatever joy you see today," I said as I gestured to my paralyzed legs, "was hard won this morning. And ladies, it's the only way to live. It's the *Christian* way to live."

I'm not the only one who needs God desperately. I'm not even the main one.

It's my husband, Ken. I know there are times—bless his heart—when he sighs under his breath, "I can't do this. I can't face another day of giving Joni exercises, getting her dressed and lifting her into the wheelchair. I've been through this routine countless times. I don't have strength or resources."

I appreciate Ken's honesty too. And I understand. Thankfully, Ken and I have sought help from friends to assist with my "get up" and "go to bed" routines. But whoever helps, that caregiver has still chosen to pass up morning coffee with a friend at the deli or has sacrificed her own schedule to accommodate mine. The caregiver faces the same day-in and day-out routine, putting one foot in front of the other, often plodding, sometimes pushing beyond human strength.

Caregivers need the smile of God too. They get tired. Their needs are often urgent and desperate. Where can helpers like my husband turn? The first step is to go to God. The next step is to pick up *A Caregiver's Survival Guide*. Kay Strom is a caregiver who has invested countless hours in helping her disabled husband. She knows what it's like to plod through the routines, and she has opened up her heart and shared her poignant and powerful account of how she "found the smile of God" through it all. Kay has experienced a lifetime of lessons and has catalogued invaluable insights to pass on to other caregivers. She has given us a book that reflects her heart, as well as a wealth of resources, advice, direction and wisdom covering every topic from guilt to guidance.

I admire people like Kay, people like my husband. No, not all caregivers face the exact same issues or decisions, but they face the same needs— spiritual ones, as well as emotional and practical.

This is why I am so happy to recommend *A Caregiver's Survival Guide*. I want you, as a caregiver, to have every resource possible. I want you to have at your disposal all the insight and direction you need. Like my husband, Ken, you are *so important* to someone like me. We need you. We appreciate you (although some of us with disabilities may not express it very well). One more thing. God appreciates you too, for he commends those who honor him by serving others in need when he says, "Is not [the way to please me] to share your food with the hungry and to provide the poor wanderer with shelter—when you see the naked, to clothe him, *and not to turn away from your own flesh and blood?*" (Isaiah 58:7, italics mine).

You haven't. You're hanging in there. And I know—I just know—you will find the smile of God. After all, he resists the proud, the self-reliant and those who insist "I don't need help," and he gives his smile to those who desperately need him.

Joni Eareckson Tada
President, Joni and Friends

Acknowledgments

I gratefully acknowledge the many people who helped me along my journey through ten years of caregiving. My parents, Albert and Marjorie Marshall, and my sisters and brothers, especially Jo Jeanne Baughn, were wonderfully supportive. Cliff and Clara Strom, my parents-in-law, reached beyond their own pain to encourage and comfort me, and to assist in more ways than I can count. My children, Lisa and Eric, and my son-in-law Arie Ringnalda, were never-wavering supporters and encouragers.

Dolly Dickenson repeatedly called me to reality and helped me to accept it. Gerda Inger never failed to be available to both Larry and me, and I thank her for her loving and caring spirit. Don Caswell was an endlessly faithful companion to Larry and a great sounding board for me. Dan Kline invested an enormous amount of time, energy and patience in making Larry's and my life as comfortable as possible. When everyone else was too busy, he made time to stay with Larry so I could get away.

I gratefully appreciate Dr. Mark Corazza who listened to me when no other doctor did, and patiently and caringly worked with Larry. What a blessing it was to have a physician who was not only the best medically, but was also a committed Christian who consistently pointed us to the Great Physician. Dr. Jim Nelson, our first minister, and his wife, Betty, offered more than comfort and encouragement—they allowed us to live in their condominium during a major part of our house rebuilding process. My present minister, Rev. Scott Bridges, and his wife, Julie, went above and beyond the call of duty to be caring friends and supporters. The members of Christ Presbyterian Church were the best of what the family of God should be.

To all of these and to so many more I gratefully and humbly say thank you.

1

There Is Something Wrong

MISFORTUNES BEFALL ALL OF US, BUT REALLY BAD THINGS ONLY HAPPEN TO other people. Deep down in our hearts, we all believe this. It's what allows us to eat and drink in spite of the warnings about germs and toxins in our environment. It's what convinces us to release our children in spite of the threats of the outside world. It's what permits us to speed along the highway at seventy miles an hour in a vehicle with a tank full of flammable gasoline. It is this assurance that lets us move through our days without being paralyzed by all the imaginable calamities that could potentially rock our world.

"I'll be all right," we assure ourselves. "My family and I will be okay."

Over time, through living together and sharing our lives, we achieve a unique kind of family familiarity. Usually it's comfortable and comforting— except when something isn't right. We can sense that. Even if we can't describe it or explain it or understand it, we can *feel* it.

That's how it was when my husband Larry's problem started. It was quiet and gradual, and it sneaked up on us. I noticed little things. In retrospect I'm sure Larry did, too, but we didn't talk about it, not until after the car accident and his cracked pelvis.

"Crazy lady driver!" Larry said.

But I wondered. One of the things I had noticed was what seemed to be increasing carelessness in his driving.

The injury wasn't too bad. He didn't need a cast, and the doctor said he would be completely healed within six weeks. But two months went by, then three, and still Larry was limping noticeably. Yet whenever I mentioned a return trip to the doctor, Larry bristled.

"I made an appointment to have that limp checked out," I finally informed him. "And I paid in advance, so you might as well go."

"Well, I don't want you to be in the doctor's office with me!" he snapped.

"Why not?" I asked. We had always gone together to any important medical appointments. We had figured four ears were better than two. What one of us missed, the other heard. What one of us forgot, the other remembered.

"Because," Larry stated, "you'll tell him something is wrong with my mind."

His mind? What did his mind have to do with his limp?

Larry canceled the appointment.

My husband had always been a good driver, but riding in the car with him became an increasingly frightening ordeal. "Stop!" I cried for what seemed like the thousandth time. "The light is red!"

"I know," he calmly replied as he slammed on the brakes and swerved onto the shoulder of the road to miss the line of stopped cars ahead of us. "No problem."

Something was wrong.

Other things were happening too. "The bank called again today," I told Larry one morning. "The manager said there are still more deposits claimed than they can account for. And she said you haven't responded to any of her other calls."

"Don't worry," he replied breezily. "The bank is always mixed up."

The *bank* was mixed up? And yet—as he repeatedly pointed out—Larry was the business manager of a large corporation. He had always been good in business matters in general and finances in particular. Still . . .

Finally I put it to him straight. "What's going on with you?" I demanded more sharply than I intended. "Why are you making so many mistakes? *What's wrong with you?*"

"There's nothing wrong with me," Larry answered calmly. "I'm fine, just fine." Then he added, *"You're* the one with the problem."

Could he be right? Nobody else seemed to be noticing anything unusual about him. At least they didn't mention it to me. I began to doubt my own judgment. And yet I was the one who knew him best, and it was becoming more and more clear to me that *something was definitely wrong!*

As the months passed, Larry grew physically more unsteady and mentally more out of touch. I dragged him to a succession of doctors, and they had a succession of ideas, from the simple ("It's just stress—he needs to take things easy for awhile") to the complicated ("It's Charcot Marie Tooth Disease"), from the benign ("A couple of sessions with a psychiatrist should take care of the problem") to the terrifying ("It could be a brain tumor"). But the doctors never seemed to agree with one another, tests never confirmed anything, and no treatment anyone suggested helped. Whatever was wrong just kept getting worse and worse and worse.

It was two years before a diagnosis was finally made—chorea acanthocytosis, an extremely rare genetic condition. It was another month, several consultations and a whole stack of medical journal articles before the impact of that diagnosis sunk in: profound physical deterioration, increasing dementia, relentless progression, untreatable, incurable, fatal . . .

I was staggered. Had there been any normalcy in our lives, it would have been shattered. As it was, we were already living chaotically. Six months earlier, while we were on our dream family vacation to England, a rampaging forest fire destroyed our neighborhood. We lost everything except the one suitcase of clothing we had taken with us. Two months later our son Eric joined his sister Lisa at college halfway across the country. We had scrambled to get things together for them. Now this diagnosis crashed in on top of our already frantic and confused existence.

"Why did this have to happen to us?" I cried out again and again. "And if it had to happen, why now?"

I have since learned that life-altering events never hit at convenient times. There is no convenient time for catastrophe.

That winter was the beginning of a frantic roller coaster ride, up through denial and down through despair, jerked around and around by anger and guilt and frustration, down through terror and up through hope.

"We'll get through this together," I assured Larry. "We've made it through so much before, we can get through this too." Breezily he answered that I was making far too much out of the whole thing. Everything would be all right in a few weeks, maybe a month or so at the most. Until then, he was going to enjoy having a break from work.

Then came the inevitable suggestions for remedies from friends, relatives and people off the street. They sounded preposterous, yet I couldn't help asking myself, *What if there really* is *a "miracle cure"? How could I live with myself if I denied Larry his one real chance to be healed?* And so the progression began.

A friend told us of a neighbor who had a friend who knew a woman who had developed a concoction of vitamins and other natural products that had cured everything from cancer to AIDS. "It's no sure thing," our friend conceded, "but it's worth a try." I was skeptical, but Larry was convinced. The pills didn't work.

A fellow who worked with Larry knew of a powdered substance that was capable of cleaning out one's entire system, thus ridding the body of all offending elements. "A thorough cleansing is all the body needs," he stated enthusiastically. "This will work for Larry. I'm sure of it!" So was Larry. But that concoction didn't work either.

A man we knew only casually informed us that he had just "received a gift of healing and casting out demons" and that God was telling him to heal Larry. Larry was positive this man was the answer. The man came, and after an hour or so stated triumphantly that he had successfully exorcised the demons and healed Larry. Then he went home assuring us that though it might take a while for the healing to be apparent, Larry would get no worse. Larry got worse.

During our twenty-five years of marriage Larry and I had faced many problems together, from minor inconveniences to what we considered major disasters. But this time was different. This time we were not facing the problem together. We were not upholding and supporting and encouraging each other. I felt that I was doing it alone while Larry blissfully went on his way, seemingly oblivious to everything. Even when he was told he couldn't return to work. Even when his driver's license was revoked. Even when the doctor told him the most he could hope to do was work in a sheltered workshop for the handicapped. "There's no real problem," Larry insisted again and again. "Pretty soon things will be back to normal."

How I missed the Larry I had grown to know so well! The practical, sensible, let's-get-to-the-bottom-of-this-and-find-an-answer Larry. The Larry I could talk to and pray with. The Larry who would talk to me.

Maybe this time I can't *make it,* I thought miserably. *Maybe this time it will be too much.*

Larry and I had always celebrated our separateness. I enjoyed writing and early morning walks along the beach and reading the classics and growing vegetables in my garden. He liked to create in his woodshop and work on the car and invest in the stock market and watch *Star Trek* reruns on television. And yet we were one. We loved doing things with the kids—traveling and camping and skiing. We enjoyed our involvement at church and getting together with friends. How strange it seemed to increasingly be just me, one person, all alone.

I read everything I could get my hands on that might possibly offer help, from medical articles to inspirational accounts of other people's experiences. But in all my reading, nothing prepared me for the emotional upheavals I would face, for the adjustments that lay ahead for every member of our family, for the desperate need I would have for an understanding ear and a strong shoulder to cry on, for the inevitable letting go of expectations. There was little to tell me what to do or who to call for help. And there was little to assure me that there were blessings to be found and islands of relief and reserves of hope available to me.

Are you a caregiver? Then come, let me walk the journey with you. Let me share from my own experience and those of others who have been down that difficult road. Let me pass along the insights they passed along to me and also those I painfully gained firsthand.

Caregiving is a journey that should not—and need not—be made alone.

2

New Role,
Uncomfortable Fit

LARRY'S LIMP WORSENED UNTIL HE WASN'T ABLE TO WALK WITHOUT A LEG BRACE. He also began losing the use of his right arm. ("It doesn't matter," he assured me airily. "I don't need that one. I'm left-handed!") An especially curious thing happened too—he lost his ability to feel pain. To Larry this was proof that nothing was seriously wrong. If it didn't hurt, it couldn't be too bad.

At times Larry's deterioration was rapid. At other times he seemed to reach a plateau and stay there for months. But then the relentless deterioration began again.

One particular November day will be etched in my mind forever. Fall had come, even to Southern California. The liquid amber trees proudly wore their autumn hues of red, orange and gold, and the air was crisp and tangy. I was sitting in the car waiting for Larry to come out of the sheltered workshop where he was working. So intent was I on the glories of the day that I didn't notice the building door open. When I looked up, I gasped out loud. Larry had gone right past the car and was out on the street corner where he was asking passersby for money. *Who is he, that twig-thin, drooling man on the corner?* I asked myself. *Could he really be my husband? That man whose every step is a struggle? Who seldom speaks more than a couple of slurred words to me? Could he be my Larry?*

If you are a caregiver, you likely are well acquainted with the crushing helplessness of such a moment of truth. Listen to what a woman named Christine* has to say:

> I remember the exact moment I became a caregiver. A man called me from the Greyhound Bus depot downtown and told me an old woman was there, confused and crying in the restroom. He said someone found my telephone number in her purse, and would I come down and get her? I couldn't figure out who he was talking about. My mother was seventy, but I didn't think of her as old. And although her memory had become a little fuzzy, I certainly wouldn't call her confused. And the Greyhound Bus depot? As far as I knew, she'd never ridden the bus in her life.
>
> But I hurried downtown, and sure enough, there was my mother. I took her arm, and she hit me in the face. My loving, sweet, ever-patient mother actually hit me!

Christine's mother, Ruth, was suffering from Alzheimer's disease—a far more common condition that chips away at the brain. For a couple of years Ruth had been struggling through the early stages of the disease, but by maintaining close parameters on her life she had managed to keep her difficulties fairly well hidden.

"She had a definite routine, and she stuck to it," Christine said. "I had no idea how essential that routine was for her."

The day of the bus depot incident Ruth had reluctantly decided to drive downtown to get a birthday gift for her granddaughter. She never got the gift. Realizing that she was becoming confused, she parked her car and decided to take the bus home. But the sounds and sights at the unfamiliar bus depot were more than she could handle.

Ruth guessed what was happening to her, and she was terrified. I'm not sure what Larry understood or how he felt. He never said. A number of times I tried talking to him about it, as did a couple of close friends, but he always acted as though he didn't know what we were talking about. Did he ever comprehend the severity of his disease? I hope not.

As for the rest of the family, we knew. And we didn't know what to say

---

*Identifying details and all names have been changed except for my family and those few—including the doctor—who gave written permission. All of the occurrences are true.

to one another, let alone to other people.

You Are Not Alone

I have never met anyone who is caring for a loved one with chorea acantho-cytosis, and I doubt if I ever will. Yet although each caregiver's story is unique, in some ways they are all alike. Many people today are struggling to provide at-home caregiving, and as our population grows older, the number will skyrocket. Consider just one cause of disability—Alzheimer's disease. Right now countless relatives and friends are providing most of the care for close to four million sufferers of this affliction. But by the middle of the next century, when people now in their twenties are elderly, the number of Alzheimer's patients is expected to leap to a staggering fourteen million—a number equal to the current population of Florida.

Add to these numbers parents who are caring for children and young adults with such conditions as Down syndrome and cerebral palsy, and adults caring for family members who have had strokes or debilitating inju-ries, or any one of a number of other incapacitating conditions. According to a survey conducted by the National Center of Health Statistics, approxi-mately ten million chronically ill Americans are living at home.

Now factor in those who have loved ones in institutions whom they visit regularly, for whom they make decisions and over whom they watch to make sure of proper and compassionate treatment. Add in family members who are struggling to stretch their lives enough to care for elderly or dis-abled parents who do not live with them, or even nearby. With today's mo-bile society, many people need to care for loved ones from a distance. While these people don't provide the direct care, they do make arrangements for it. Whether they live nearby or not, their loved ones are in their hearts and on their minds.

Help!

Caregivers are a largely neglected legion of millions whose lives have been put on hold (at best) or completely shattered (at worst) when they were suddenly and unexpectedly thrust into the role of perpetual guardian.

"Relentless, that's what it is," sobbed a weary seventy-three-year-old woman whose husband suffers from Parkinson's disease. "It's a round-the-clock job, and I am exhausted!"

And every setback or complication leads to a downward spiral of despair.

"What can I do about my parents?" asked Paul, a forty-eight-year-old husband and father of four. "They live on the other side of the country, yet they are constantly calling me to do things I can't possibly do for them."

"My brother is in a nursing home in Oklahoma, and I live in Florida," said Sandy, a single businesswoman. "He has no one to look out for him, but I am so far away. How much can I do?"

An older couple who had left the mission field years earlier because of the needs of their disabled son lamented, "We hoped that eventually he would be able to live independently, but it's clear that he will always need someone. We're getting older and are having our own health problems. What will happen to our boy when we can no longer care for him?"

Helpless. That one word sums up the way we too often feel. Physically and emotionally helpless. And the fact that the old, familiar roles no longer work accentuate that helplessness.

Old Roles, Wrong Fit

Larry had always been in charge of the finances in our family. It was an obvious fit; he was the business person. He paid the bills and did most of the banking. Now, with the latest bills and bank statements ashes in the mailbox of our burned home, and with all our records gone, Larry was hopelessly confused and befuddled. He couldn't make sense of anything financial. And since he could no longer continue at his job, our primary income had come to an abrupt halt. Both of our two cars had been destroyed in the fire, and Larry wasn't up to wise car shopping. Yet he held tenaciously to his old business manager roles.

I was so overwhelmed that I desperately clung to the hope that Larry could still do what he had once done. He couldn't. I could not understand why the man who was supposed to be my partner was acting more and more like a difficult child. The person I counted on to be the head of our family, the one to lead us, no longer knew the way. And I didn't know how to take his place. Nor did I want to learn.

Old roles no longer fit, and new ones hang awkwardly on our caregiver shoulders.

My friend Toni, caregiver for her mother, remembers exactly when this realization hit her. "As I helped my mother to the bathroom, I suddenly un-

Can we get around this shifting of roles? Probably not. But some things may help adjust the uncomfortable fit.

- *Encourage your loved one to express his feelings.* It can be extremely difficult for your loved one to admit he needs your help. He is almost certainly confused and frightened by the physical and mental changes in himself, and he may go to extreme lengths to keep from having to admit to those changes.

  Try to ease some of his anxiety by reassuring him. At times this can be accomplished with words, and at other times you will need to find other ways. Larry was afraid of the doctor and especially of having his blood pressure taken. I could tell when he was frightened because his ticks and spasms worsened. That was my clue to comfort him by reading to him. It didn't matter what I read, just the cadence of my voice calmed him down.

  However your loved one is able to communicate his feelings, be there to hear him. Let him know you understand it's hard to accept the limitations and that it must be terribly frustrating to have to deal with them. If he has a suggestion as to what you can do to help, let him know you are willing to try. Even if there is nothing specific you can do, just being there and caring will likely be comforting. And letting him know you have time for him, and that his feelings matter to you, can go a long way toward helping him be able to share his concerns with you.

- *Help the person stay connected.* Whatever your loved one's condition, she needs to feel she is still an important part of the family. If possible, also help her remain a part of the church and the community. Encourage friends, people from the church and family members to visit, even if only for a brief time. Remind those who live a distance away to keep in touch with regular telephone calls, letters and cards. And encourage your loved one to socialize with others in whatever way and to whatever degree is appropriate.

  Feeling she no longer has anything to contribute, your loved one may become withdrawn and isolated. Try giving her a subscription to the local newspaper or to a favorite magazine. (*Reader's Digest* was great for Larry.) Read it with her so you can talk about it together. Take her on a walk outside and enjoy God's creation. Drive to the beach and listen together as the waves crash on the shore. Take her to see the spring flowers in bloom, or to enjoy the colors of the autumn leaves or the bright display of Christmas lights. And, if it is at all possible, make sure your loved one is able to get to worship services.

- *Allow your loved one to be as independent and in control as possible.* Yes, independence and control are elusive. But do all you can to make your loved one's environment as comfortable, familiar and controllable as possible. Let him have a say in how his living area is furnished, and let him decide where to place his belongings. And please, please, talk things over with him. Even if he can't make the actual decisions about his life, consult him before you make decisions that affect him. It won't always be possible, but whenever you can, respect his preferences and opinions. Encourage him to make whatever choices and decisions he is able to make.

Yes, it is often easier to just take over and do everything yourself. But if you make the conscious effort to allow a little extra time so the person in your care can participate, it makes a huge difference in how he feels about himself—and how he feels about you.

- *Be attentive to your loved one's spiritual needs.*

   "Why me?"

   "Does God know what's happening to me?"

   "Does he care?"

How do you answer questions like these? It's difficult, especially when you are asking the same questions yourself! But don't get caught in the trap of trying to defend God and his actions. The basic fact is that, whether it seems like it or not, God is in control, and he does do all things well. Instead of trying to give your loved one answers, look back with her and help her recall the moments of blessings and joy in her life. Encourage her to remember the times she saw God's hand at work. Read passages of Scripture that assure her of God's undying love and care. (One of our favorites was Romans 8:31-39:"If God is for us, who can be against us? . . . Neither death nor life, neither angels nor demons, neither the present nor the future, nor any powers, neither height nor depth, nor anything else in all creation, will be able to separate us from the love of God that is in Christ Jesus our Lord.")

Encourage your loved one to talk about her plans and hopes, even if you know they are unrealistic. (Larry talked of going to the university and becoming a veterinarian. What did it hurt to send off for an application for him?) Be supportive by listening well even though you may have heard the same thing over and over again. ("I'll take care of cats and dogs, maybe even birds and rabbits. But only well ones, not sick ones.") Demonstrate patience by being patient, love by being loving, care by really caring.

Your loved one may talk of feelings of guilt, regret or anger from the past. Ask if she wants you to write a letter to someone for her or to buy a card she can send. Offer to pray with her. Remind her of God's great forgiveness. Psalm 130:3-4 assures us:

> If you, O LORD, kept a record of sins,
> O LORD, who could stand?
> But with you there is forgiveness.

If you are too close to the situation, arrange to have someone else pray with her and help her. You might ask your minister or a representative from your church.

derstood that we were moving through an important passage. The mother who had cared for my needs when I could not help myself was now in need of the same care from me. I didn't do anything for her that she wouldn't have done for me. Only she would have done it without grumbling, because I was her child."

Taking on new roles can be terribly painful, but no less so than relinquishing the old ones. While I staggered under an increasingly heavy load, Larry was forced to watch his own role crumbling away. Doing everything alone was exhausting, but it was also crushing to see Larry's confusion and frustration as he lost one part of his life after another. (*"Why* can't I get a power saw? What do you mean I shouldn't be driving? I want to be in charge of the insurance money! Why can't I?")

Caregivers have no choice but to take over and do more. Yet the more we take over and do and accomplish, the more alone and ignored and unappreciated our loved ones feel. It's a cruel cycle.

As Positive and Pain Free as Possible
Role changes are going to happen. And no, neither of you is going to like it. The challenge is to make the changes as painless and positive as you possibly can.

It will help to know where your loved one is in the course of the disability, and to have some idea of what's coming. Because Larry's condition was so rare and so little was known about it—no doctor in our area had ever seen a case before—no one was able to give much information. But even if your loved one is afflicted with something relatively well known and predictable, her situation will be specific to her. There just is no such thing as "one size fits all."

But It's So Hard
There aren't any simple answers or easy solutions. That's the nature of chronic illness and disability.

For caregivers, it's so hard because we miss the people our loved ones once were, and we mourn all that they will never have the chance to be. Then, too, we wonder if we can ever do all that needs to be done.

"I know myself," one man said. "I can make only so many sacrifices without becoming bitter and resentful."

Answering these questions will help you understand the inevitable role changes and begin planning for what lies ahead:

1. What roles have you had to take over from your loved one?

2. Have you asked his or her doctor to give you instructions and guidance, both verbally and in writing?

3. Are there specific approaches you can take that will make the changes easier for you? How about for your loved one?

4. What roles will you likely have to assume as time goes on?

5. What steps can you take now to prepare and smooth the way for those coming changes?

6. Are there areas in which you can allow your loved one more independence and control?

7. Have you encouraged your loved one to communicate his or her feelings and desires to you?

8. Are there nonverbal communications you need to acknowledge?

9. Is there someone besides you who can listen to and pray with your loved one?

10. Understanding that there are situations in which you are not the best person to deal with the one in your care, is there someone else you can call on?

That's good. It's important for us to know our limits. Yet it is even more important that we trust God to carry us to our limit and then beyond it. Ask him for his compassion. Ask him for his strength. Ask him for his grace. Approach his throne of grace with confidence so that you may receive mercy and find grace to help you in your time of need (see Hebrews 4:16).

Ask on behalf of your loved one. Ask on your own behalf. And ask on behalf of your entire family, for they are all affected.

3

The Entire Family
Is Affected

MY CHILDREN DON'T KNOW THE MAN I MARRIED. THEY THINK THEY REMEMBER their father, but I know they don't. The change in him was so insidious and sneaky, and over time so thoroughly overwhelming, that even I have difficulty remembering the caring man Larry once was, with all his excitement for life and his hopes and dreams for the future.

Chorea acanthocytosis doesn't strike its victims, it creeps up and engulfs them. Then slowly, silently, it tightens its grip and smothers the person's memory, reasoning, judgment and even personality. In hindsight, the doctors count back to the first sign of onset—a seizure Larry suffered at work. Lisa was ten at the time and Eric was eight. But it wasn't until six years later that I began to suspect that the changes I was noticing might be more than "stubbornness," "eccentricities" or "orneriness." It was another two years before doctors started investigating and still another year before the condition was identified. By then Lisa was in college, and Eric was finishing high school.

For almost ten years we all experienced a steady decline we didn't even know was taking place.

One day, after weeping on the telephone with the children at college in Michigan, I went to dinner with friends who had a twenty-six-year-old schizophrenic son. My tears started again, and we all cried together.

"Forgive me," I sniffled. "I shouldn't be dumping on you. Your situation is worse than mine. Your Matt never had a chance for a life. At least Larry had that."

"No," they insisted, "your situation is worse. We have each other to lean on, but you have to deal with it alone."

Neither of us was right, and neither was wrong. No one's situation is better or worse than another's. It's all crummy, and it's crummy for the entire family. Each family member has to adjust to the new situation in his or her own way. Each must learn to cope with its stresses. Family members can help and encourage one another, but it takes time and patience and understanding, things that are in short supply in a caregiving household.

Don't Burden the Kids

"Our problems are adult problems," insisted a father of three, the youngest of whom suffers from a whole range of debilitating birth defects. "The strains are mainly financial, although I'll admit the stress is spilling over into our marriage. But the children can't do anything about those problems, so why pull them into it?"

There's no need to pull them. They are already in it.

For some caregivers, the hands-on care can be so consuming that the only time they touch their children is to meet their physical needs. There is neither time nor emotional energy for love pats or snuggles or spontaneous hugs. But even for the young ones, there is a positive side. There are responsibilities, sensitivities and awarenesses that only a child raised in a caregiving household can learn and experience. And although it can be tough, it can also be a real blessing.

Financial and emotional strains are not confined to just one person or even to the adults. They impact the entire family. Children find themselves competing for time and attention. With finances strained, they can easily feel deprived. Many children—especially teenagers—are thrust into the position of having to assume a greater amount of the housework and even caregiving responsibilities. What affects the parents affects the kids.

"I have children, and I have a husband with advanced multiple sclerosis," said an exhausted thirty-six-year-old mother of three elementary school-age children. "And I'll be honest—my husband requires far more time and energy than half a dozen children!" Then, with tears flowing, she added, "Imagine what it's like for the kids. They know their daddy isn't going to get better. Angela, my oldest, used to insist on praying that he would get well. Now she just says, 'What's the use?' It breaks my heart."

For the children of a sick parent who has no hope for recovery, life is often a series of dashed hopes, impossible dreams, painful memories and seemingly unanswered prayers. Cruel taunts from other children who don't understand just add to their pain and confusion.

You say you just don't have time to meet your children's needs? Then think about enlisting the help of others. Here are some ideas:

- Suggest that friends and relatives take the children for a day and do something fun with them: go out for hamburgers, visit the zoo, go shopping, have a picnic.

- Encourage your kids to be kids. Let them experience the good things they once took for granted—eating out, going to the movies, wrestling on the living room floor.

- Encourage small doses of frivolity, such as suggesting they order a hot fudge sundae instead of a nutritious snack.

- Enroll them in after-school activities that develop their interests and talents.

- Take a few minutes each day to listen, one on one, to each of your children. Encourage them to share about their activities.

- Let your children see that it's all right to ask the questions on their minds and to share their concerns with you.

- Be honest about financial constraints. Kids cannot cooperate when they aren't aware of what is going on.

- Be truthful about the prognosis. If it's certain—short of a miracle—say so. If it's an unpredictable disease, one that can worsen suddenly and then go into remission, explain that. It is easier to deal with a hard truth than to be left hanging and guessing.

- Acknowledge the extra burden your children have to carry.

- Be alert to the emotional stresses of your young people—for instance, they may see the ill person as monopolizing everyone's attention.

- Ask caring people of God to encircle your children with daily prayer.

Please, caregiver, find a way to let your children be children. Encourage their artistic, athletic and musical abilities. Think long and hard before you decide to "protect" them from the realities of the situation. Knowing the truth from you will likely be easier on them than worrying and guessing about the unknown.

Help Them Adapt and Accept

For several years Larry was able to work at a sheltered workshop with other adults who suffered from a variety of brain impairments. One day someone from our church saw him shuffling and stumbling along the street after work. It didn't take long for the whispered gossip to get back to our son: "Your father was downtown *drunk!*"

Eric could not change the facts of his father's condition any more than your children can change the facts of what is affecting their loved one. Help them come to where they can accept what is occurring and to adapt to it as best they can. Sometimes that may mean correcting a misconception about the disabled person. (My son explained, "My dad's not drunk, he has a disease.") Other times that isn't possible.

The best way you can help your children accept and adapt is by modeling acceptance and adaptation. So first of all, examine yourself: *What do you do when one of your children is hurt, upset or embarrassed by your loved one's appearance or behavior in public?* It's important to acknowledge your child's feelings. Don't scold or shame him, or accuse him of being unloving, uncaring or un-Christian. Encourage him to talk with you about his feelings, but remind him that the disabled person has feelings too. More important than anything you say is the way your child sees you responding with loving, patient decorum during those awkward moments.

This is a good opportunity to remind your child of a very important biblical concept—God does not see things the way humans do. People look at the outward appearance, but God looks on the heart (see 1 Samuel 16:6-7).

What are some of the ways your family is coping with the disability? If you cannot think of any, perhaps you need to get out a pen and paper and write down some specifics.

How do you encourage your kids to pitch in and help? Have you

3 0 ———————————— A Caregiver's Survival Guide

thought out responses to their most well-used excuses? Being a part of the team helps them to have a vested interest in both the difficult times and the times of success.

"But," you may say, "my children are really young. I don't think they are even affected by the situation at home."

Don't be so sure. Children who have a chronically ill or dying family member experience all the emotions you experience. And those emotions are compounded by fear, isolation, anger and often guilt. If your children are old enough to love, they are old enough to grieve.

Certainly each child in your family is special and individual. Whatever the age, each one requires special and individual care to help him or her emerge into adulthood stronger for having been raised in a caregiving family.

Listen to Francine's story:

> My father was always sickly and in and out of hospitals. He died when I was sixteen. As the oldest of three children, it was up to me to run the family printing business. My two brothers married and moved away, but I felt I needed to stay and take care of my mother who is badly crippled with arthritis. It was so hard, but who could I complain to? My mom felt bad enough the way it was, and I certainly can't blame my brothers for going on with their lives. I'm now twenty-two, and I still run the business, the house and take care of my mom. People tell me I am so strong. I had dreamed of going to college, and when I realized that wasn't going to happen, I wondered what would happen to me. My mother tells me I'm wonderful and that she couldn't get by without me. My friends think I'm indestructible. I know I'm not wonderful, and I'm certainly not indestructible. But God has been good to me. The business is going well, Mom is holding her own, and I am dating a really sweet, caring man. I'm not sure what the future holds, but I no longer feel like I'm on a sinking ship.

Old age, and the disabilities that accompany it, can be difficult and confusing for children. We think of grandmas and grandpas as being jolly, kindly souls, gentle and sweet-tempered. But that's not always the case.

One woman lamented, "People are always telling me, 'Your children and grandchildren must give your husband so much to live for.' How little they know! My husband is so absorbed in his illness that he has no energy left for anyone or anything else. He only thinks about us when he wants something from us."

Too often we assume that our family members, including the children and teens, will just naturally, somehow, understand and appreciate what's going on. It doesn't happen that way. That's why it's important, whenever possible and appropriate, to make a specific effort to include your children and other family members in discussions. They need to know what is happening and what to expect.

"My children avoid my elderly father-in-law," one mother of an adolescent and two teenagers shared. "Gramps doesn't live with us, but I go over every day to cook and clean and visit. I know it hurts him that the children never come, but they insist that 'he creeps us out.' He can be difficult, I know, and he is practically deaf, so it's hard to communicate with him. I want my children to know their grandfather, but I don't know how to convince them to come along with me to see him."

Unless young people are exposed to older folks in the right way, they can tend to view the aged as silly, useless and uncomfortable to be around. It's a sad and unfortunate stereotype.

As a young person is around an older person, the tie between them will grow and the discomfort will decrease.

Family at a Distance

It is easy to see how an illness affects children, teens and other family members who live with the person needing care. Even when the loved one is next door or down the street or across town. But what about those who live a long distance away? Can they be considered caregivers, too?

Paul, a computer technician in his fifties, says, "Absolutely! Even though my sisters live near my parents, they refuse to take any responsibility for them. I live all the way across the country, but I'm the one Dad calls when they have a problem. And those problems are becoming more and more frequent."

Providing care from a distance has it's own challenges and difficulties. On his third emergency flight across the country—his almost deaf father had been in an automobile accident—Paul decided he had to get some help. A local agency he contacted gave him the telephone number for Senior Connection. The people there gave him advice about legal and financial issues, and they referred him to legal counseling. Paul contacted the Department of Motor Vehicles about his father's driving and arranged for him to have a driving test. He also got in touch with a care-management service. For an hourly fee a manager assessed his parents' situation and determined their ongoing needs.

Paul also called his sisters. "They have legitimate issues with my parents," Paul concedes. He didn't scold or accuse them. He simply told them that if they were ever going to work toward healing those old hurts, they would need to take the initiative, and the sooner the better. When he assured his sisters that they wouldn't have to take over their parents' care, both agreed to have contact with them. Through the nationwide Eldercare Locator, Paul found a Christian counselor who was willing to help his sisters and their parents take a biblical approach to working out their difficulties.

"I started the process while I was back in Virginia," Paul said, "but I could have done the same thing from my home in Oregon. Now my wife and I go back on a *scheduled* basis, and to visit my parents, not just to handle emergencies."

Young people will find it easier to be with the elderly if they have something specific to do. Here are some ideas:

- Take something to read aloud.
- Water the plants.
- Take photographs to look at together.
- Ask the older person to share events from the past.
- Perform. (If the young person is taking music lessons, he might play a piece. She could recite a poem or try out the magic act she is doing in the school talent show. He can show off his artwork.)
- Share a hobby.
- Bring a small pet the two can enjoy together.
- Take along a game to play together. (Checkers is my personal favorite.)
- Do a task. (Mow the lawn, dust the furniture, bake brownies.)
- Put up seasonal decorations. (And, of course, take them down afterward!)

Appreciate Each Person

Near or far, young or old, everyone in your family is affected. Because everyone's role may have changed to one extent or another, do all you can to make certain that the new roles are appropriate. Never ever communicate to a child that you expect him or her to try to take the place of a parent. It may sound noble in a movie, but in real life never say such things as, "Now, Son, you are the man of the family" or "You'll have to be Mama now." Children cannot and should not be expected to fill parents' shoes. Look at the unique place every member of your family fills and appreciate each for what he or she contributes.

If Grandma reads to the disabled person, say, "Thank you for reading. It is such an important part of his day."

If your teen picks up an audiocassette of a book at the public library, tell him, "How kind of you to think of that. Could you bring home new ones on a regular basis?"

If your child picks up her toys and hangs up her clothes, tell her, "I appreciate it so much. Thank you for making my day easier."

Even while you are juggling far more than you ever thought you could, it is vital that you keep your home a safe harbor for your family. Provide for them a sanctuary where every one of you has a special opportunity to see God at work.

They Are More Resilient Than You Think

It was on June 27, 1990, a sweltering summer evening, when huge flames roared down the canyon from the mountains behind Santa Barbara. Fueled by seventy-mile-an-hour winds, they leveled homes, leaped the freeway and left a charred wasteland in their path. When my family and I stood in the ashes of what had been our house and gazed out at the devastation, I shook my head and cried, "Total destruction! It will be years before this place will look anywhere near normal again." But before our new foundation was even poured, sprouts of hearty bougainvillea and the lacy leaves of California poppies poked their heads up through the scorched ground. Soon there were leaves and fronds on the tops of blackened palm trees. By the time our house was framed, wild rabbits were hopping through the yard, nibbling at the growing greenery. The day we moved back in—a year and a half after the fire—a long, brown roadrunner plucked up a lizard and ran through the grasses and wildflowers of our unlandscaped yard, stopping just long enough to peer in at me through the sliding glass door.

Ah, the resilience of nature. How I had underestimated the power of a small seed!

When disasters roar through our families, destroying everything comfortable and familiar, and laying waste to what we hold dear, we cry out in despair, "Nothing will ever be right again!"

But we underestimate God. Even in our times of great pain and loss, God's power is at work in the lives of his children. You can trust him with your family. Ask him for strength, guidance and wisdom. Ask him to grow up a hedge of protection around your young ones. Give their cries of anger and frustration and despair over to him.

He will not let you down.

He will not let go of your family.

4

Crushing Emotions

MENTAL DETERIORATION BRINGS WITH IT A SPECIAL PAIN. IT CAN CHANGE A CARING family member into a nasty, suspicious—even violent—stranger. This "stranger" in my house became more and more frightening to me. Whenever I started to take a shower, he would stand outside and whisper threats. It was particularly unnerving because he did it with a smile on his face. If I locked the bathroom door, he would break things in the bedroom until I unlocked it. So it became increasingly rare that I had the luxury of more than a quick wash in the sink.

For days on end Larry would refuse to get into the car and accompany me to the grocery store; yet I didn't dare leave him home alone. So I waited until we were desperate for groceries, then I bribed him with candy and comic books to sit quietly on the floor of the supermarket while I ran through and grabbed a few things.

One day, grungy and exhausted, I was hurriedly bagging up some fresh produce when a woman I knew from church touched me on the arm. "Kay," she said, "your husband is pulling things off the shelf in aisle five."

I sat down on the floor and cried.

I can understand why caregivers snap emotionally. I was just about there myself. Already feeling powerless and stretched beyond endurance, I was certain that just one more thing would knock me over the edge.

"I admit it," said Joanne, the mother of ten-year-old Sam and his five-year-old sister, Tanya, who has Down syndrome. "I'm not proud of it, but I do admit it. I've called my son some awful things. I said he was stupid and lazy and a pain to me. I know it just destroys him, but I can't help myself. My weariness and frustration turn to anger, and I take it out on Sammy. I blurt out awful things, and then I can't take them back."

"All I ever seem to do is talk on the telephone," said a young woman whose critically ill mother had just moved in with the family. "I talk to this doctor and that doctor. I talk to people at the hospital, the social worker, the health aide. I talk to the insurance people and the Medicare people. When I'm not on the phone, I take care of my mother. I know I'm not making all the right decisions. And I feel guilty about not being there for my husband and not giving enough time to my job. I feel guilty about everything!"

"Is it normal to constantly be overwhelmed?" one woman asked. "There must have been a time when I could just go about my life and do things, then go to bed at night and sleep, but I can't remember it."

Hopeless.

Exhausted.

Frustrated.

Humiliated.

Angry.

Guilty.

Overwhelmed.

What do these all have in common? They are all feelings shared by caregivers. No matter how much you love the person you're caring for, you are human and you will have negative emotions. That's a given. The question is, what will you *do* with those emotions? Sit in the aisle of the grocery store and cry? Strike out at your healthy child? Take it out on your disabled loved one? Stifle it within you and keep right on going until you have a mental breakdown? There has to be a better way.

Crushing Emotions

Let's look at nine of the most destructive—and most common—emotions that engulf caregivers.

1. Fear

"What if she doesn't get better?"

"What if we have to get along without him?"

"What if there never again is any sense of normal for us?"

Caregivers can "what if" themselves into an early grave. We fear the unknown, and that fear can render us helpless.

2. Sadness

"I'm sad for what I've lost."

"I'm sad for what could have been, for what should have been."

"I cry over our dashed plans and hopes and dreams."

It's hard not to be sad when you remember looking into the eyes of your newborn and dreaming of all she would be before you knew the truth. It's hard not to be sad when you see the elderly couple strolling hand in hand and your spouse no longer recognizes you. It's hard not be sad when you think of your dreams of traveling to exciting places, dancing until dawn, going on ski vacations with the family, and now you know that none of that is to be.

3. Guilt

"I'm not doing enough."

"I'm not being fair to everyone."

"It should be me instead of him."

Every caregiver feels guilty. We all suspect we aren't doing a good enough job. It's difficult to allow ourselves to be less than perfect. Most of us are plagued by "survivor's guilt" ("Why isn't it me?"). We get frustrated and angry at the disabled person, and that makes us feel guiltier than ever.

4. Anger

"I have no life!"

"No one cares about *me!*"

"It isn't fair!"

Anger comes from many different sources, and it can be directed in different ways: at the disabled person, at the person who caused the accident (or at least the one who was there when it happened), at yourself, even at God. We feel angry at the disruption of our lives, at the enormous financial drain, at pity that comes our way instead of the compassion we crave, at the doctors who can't fix the problem.

5. Blame

"It's your fault! I told you not to (eat that, drink that, listen to that, stay up late) when you were expecting."

"It's my fault. I should have been there for him."

"God is punishing me by letting this happen."

Larry always told me it was my fault he was sick. Was he right? Did I put too much stress on him? Should I have been more nurturing? Was my spiritual life lax? Did I fail to pray enough? Did I not have enough faith?

Later, even when it was confirmed that Larry had a true organic disease and no one was to blame, the nagging blame continued to echo from the back of my mind. Irrational? Sure, but still it was very much there.

Blame is human. If something is wrong, someone has to be at fault. If we don't place the blame elsewhere, we just might buy into the idea that our loved one's condition really is our own doing somehow.

6. Frustration

"I can't handle his outbursts!"

"I work and work, and instead of thanks all I get is criticism."

"I am worn out, but I can't rest because she needs me."

Caregiving is filled with frustration. No matter how hard we try, no matter how diligently we work, no matter how fast we go, our lives are out of control. We feel like hamsters on exercise wheels; we run and run and run and run, but we get nowhere.

7. Depression

"I can't stop crying."

"Why do I keep trying? It's a hopeless situation."

"I go to bed at night and pray that I won't wake up."

It is so easy for caregivers to become hopeless and depressed. We are relentlessly being pushed into a reality we don't want to face.

8. Resentment

"Why him?"

"Why me?"

"It isn't fair!"

We look at other families, and since we cannot see the hurts and heartaches, we assume there are none. Our resentment boils over: "Why does it have to happen to us?"

And then there are all those who rush over to advise, "What you should do is . . ." And those who think they understand our situations, even though we know they have no clue. They are the ones who are quick to say, "You are so fortunate that he is so good (happy, helpful, loving, positive, sweet)!" We smile and nod, but we resent it because all the time we are thinking, *If you only knew!*

9. Loneliness

"I am all alone."

"No one can ever know how I feel."

"Nothing will ever fill this empty place in my heart."

After twenty-five years together it's hard to suddenly realize you are alone. "You're fortunate to still have him with you," people would say. But that was the problem; he *wasn't* still here. Not really. We used to be a couple, but now it was just me. We used to be Mom and Dad; now it was just Mom. We used to make decisions together; now I made them alone. There was no longer anyone to confide in, to share with, to make plans with, to pray with. There was no one to cry with, no one to hold me and assure me that it would be all right.

I was alone.

Caregiving is a lonely spot to be in.

It's Okay to Feel

"Snap out of it!"

"Count your blessings."

"Keep a stiff upper lip."

"Be strong."

"In whatever state you are, be content."

"Dwell on the positive."

With such admonitions coming from all sides, how dare we think—let alone say—"Hey, I'm tired of this! I'm angry and frustrated and lonely, and I hate it!"? How can we indulge our own emotions when our afflicted loved ones can't walk or maybe even think straight? How can we long for fuller lives when theirs are so constricted? How can we look at them and then allow ourselves to feel *anything* about ourselves?

Feelings of frustration and anger are normal. Even the guilt that follows them is normal. These feelings don't mean you are selfish and uncaring. In fact, they can actually be useful. Take them as reminders that you need to take a break. See them as warnings that it is important to make a point of seeking some pleasure for yourself.

Selfish? Not at all. You need to allow yourself the opportunity to become renewed and emotionally regenerated so that you can continue being a steady caregiver. As my children used to caution me: "Please, Mom, be careful. We don't want two sick parents."

Give yourself credit for doing the best you can. Allow yourself to be human. Give yourself a break and some positive strokes for what you are contributing to your loved one's care. Thank God that he has graciously allowed you the physical and inner strength to carry on, but recognize, too, that for his own divine reasons, he also gave you limits. (Read the story of Joseph in Genesis 37—45. My favorite verse in the entire account is where Joseph assures his betraying brothers, "You meant it for evil, but God meant it for good.")

Don't hesitate to step back a bit and allow yourself to see your situation from a distance.

There are certain givens in each of our situations over which we have little control. They vary from caregiver to caregiver, but for each of us there are those things we have to accept as just the way things are. There are other stresses, however, about which we can do something. The problem is to determine which are which and then to take the appropriate action.

How do you allow yourself distance? Try

* *Talking.* Not only is it okay to have feelings, it is also okay to express them. Find a safe person who will let you vent, then do it.
* *Finding an outlet.* Work in the garden. Watch birds. Take photographs. Write poetry. Do whatever allows you an escape hatch. (Reading psalms or other passages from the Bible is an excellent outlet. Even more, it will refresh you spiritually.)
* *Reshaping your dreams to fit reality.* The most destructive emotion of all is hopelessness.
* *"Blooming where you're planted."* I know, I know, it's a sappy cliché. But it's still good philosophy.

External Stresses, Internal Stresses

Stresses come in two varieties: external and internal. External stresses are the ones thrust upon you. They are more likely to be the "givens"—the things over which you have little control. For instance, the very fact that you are a caregiver is an external stress. Internal stresses, on the other hand, come from within you. They are the ones you are more likely to be able to lessen, maybe even eliminate completely.

When I sat down and listed my top external and internal stresses, my list looked like this:

External Stresses

1. Caring for Larry.
2. Larry's psychological needs and demands.
3. Getting the house rebuilt and furnished, and moving into it.
4. Taking responsibility for the family finances.
5. Assuming insurance responsibilities.
6. Meeting writing deadlines that would bring an income for the family.
7. Handling the demands and needs of other family members and my church.

Internal Stresses

1. My need to drive myself to do everything right.

2. Guilt when I fail to be perfect.
3. My own need for love and acceptance.
4. My difficulty in saying "no."
5. My tendency to take on too much and try to do it all.
6. Trying too hard to please everyone, not to offend or upset anyone.

What are your external stresses? What are your internal stresses? Sit down and make a list of each.

Now look back at your lists. Are there stresses you can eliminate? If so, check them off. Are there ones you can modify? Write out specifically how you will do that. Here is how I evaluated my lists. (The starred items are the ones I can modify, and with each of those I list my plan for doing so.)

External Stresses

1. Caring for Larry (*still on my list*).
2. Larry's psychological needs and demands (*still on my list*).
3. **Getting the house rebuilt and furnished, and moving into it. (*This doesn't have to all be done right now. Concentrate on getting the architect and a contractor. Furnishings can come much later and don't need to be done all at once.*)
4. Taking responsibility for the family finances (*still on my list*).
5. **Insurance responsibilities. (*Larry's dad is an insurance representative. I can ask him for help on this. [For you, perhaps there is someone in your church who can help.]*)
6. **Meeting writing deadlines that will bring an income for the family. (*Some of those deadlines can be renegotiated. It would mean a lower immediate income, but the lessened stress might be worth it.*)
7. **Demands and needs of other family members and of the church. (*I can ask for a leave of absence from my church obligations yet continue to attend and be as active as I can be. And I can be forthcoming about what I can and cannot do for other people. In fact, I can ask some of them to help me out now and then with Larry.*)

Internal Stresses

1. **My need to drive myself to do everything right. (*This is my prob-

lem. I need to accept that I cannot now and never will be able to do everything right.)
2. **Guilt when I fail to be perfect. *(Making some adjustments on the seventh external stress will automatically help here.)*
3. **My own need for love and acceptance. *(I can accept the love that is offered me from my children, Larry's and my families, friends, others in church and most of all from the unconditional love of God. I must release my cry for a loving response from Larry. He is unable to give it. As for acceptance, since I will never make everyone happy, it is my responsibility to do the best I can with God's help. If others are not satisfied, that's their problem, not mine.)*
4. **My difficulty in saying "no." *(I no longer have this luxury. I have to force myself to say no, even to good and worthwhile things. I cannot take on any more.)*
5. **My tendency to take on too much and try to do it all. *(It is arrogance on my part to think I can do everything better than another person, or that if I don't do it, it won't be done right.)*
6. **Trying too hard to please everyone, not to offend or upset anyone. *(It is impossible! Acknowledge it and move on.)*

What points can you check off your list? Where can you modify? Take some time with your list. Pray over it. Seek the counsel of others who know you well. Trust the Lord to guide you.

Prioritize

"First things first," the old adage advises us. Then what are the first things that you should put first? That depends. This is where the crucial task of setting priorities comes in. Which concerns should get your greatest attention? Which can wait awhile? What are the matters you will put off until you can do them without overloading your stress tolerance?

When I went over my list, I gave the highest priority to taking care of Larry and handling the finances. The next priority was given to making a living via those book deadlines. Certain house decisions had to be made, but others could be put off. I decided that furnishing the house was a low priority. We would do it whenever we could get to it.

But I Should . . .

"Shoulds" are killers. Toss them aside.

"What do you mean?" you may ask. "Everything on my list is something I *should* do. I can't just let everything go."

No, of course you can't. But you can eliminate the things you think you should do *simply because you should do them*. Let me show you what I mean:

I Think I Should . . .

☐ be an unfailing model of generosity, consideration, dignity, courage and unselfishness

☐ be a perfect lover, friend, parent, spouse

☐ be an inspiration to all who encounter me

☐ endure any hardship and pain joyfully and without complaint

☐ trust God with never a question or doubt

☐ see a godly reason for any suffering or trial in my life

☐ be able to find a solution to every problem

☐ never feel hurt, discouraged or downhearted

☐ understand everything and foresee any possible pitfall

☐ never feel "bad" emotions such as anger and jealousy

☐ always love my disabled charge with unconditional love

☐ never lose my patience

☐ never make mistakes

☐ be totally self-reliant, even while my lips are speaking of trusting in God

☐ always be at peak performance and efficiency

☐ never hurt or disappoint anyone

Those "shoulds" certainly take on a new face when we see them printed out. What I *really* should do is take that list and toss it in the wastebasket. In its place let's make another list.

With God's Help I Will . . .

☐ take one day at a time

☐ remind myself that my emotions are normal and okay

☐ love to the best of my ability

☐ resolve not to take my charge's behavior personally
☐ trust in the Lord with all my heart and not lean on my own understanding (see Proverbs 3:5)
☐ strive to acknowledge him in all my ways, and trust him to direct my path (see Proverbs 3:6)
☐ daily look to God's Word for help

Jesus, in his humanity, was well acquainted with emotions. He wept over the death of his dear friend Lazarus. He wept over Jerusalem. He wept in the garden of Gethsemene. Even when we are well aware of God's great power within us, even when we are certain of our hope for all eternity, the trials and hurts of this world can be terrible. Of course we have emotions. And with his own tears Jesus showed us that it is all right to feel. Ultimately, however, it is up to each one of us to decide what we will do with our emotions. Will we respond with anger? With self-pity? With bitterness? With resignation? Or will we in faith turn our situation, and the emotions that arise from it, over to God? Will we trust him, and through our helplessness, seek to know him better?

Such faith and trust are not always easy to come by. One of the best ways to help me get there is by turning to God's Word. Here are some verses that have helped me. Perhaps they will help you too.

Are you hurting? Find comfort here:
☐ Deuteronomy 8:1-5
☐ Psalm 77
☐ Romans 8:12-17
☐ Romans 8:35-39
Are you struggling with anger? Consider these passages:
☐ Psalm 4:4
☐ Matthew 18:21-35
☐ Ephesians 4:26-32
☐ James 1:19-20
Are you tempted to be bitter? Look to these Scriptures for help:
☐ 1 Corinthians 13
☐ Ephesians 4:29—5:2
☐ Hebrews 12:14-15

Does the future seem hopeless? Read these reassuring words:
- ☐ Isaiah 54:1-5
- ☐ Lamentations 3:19-24
- ☐ 1 Corinthians 15:20-26
- ☐ 1 Peter 1:3-9
- ☐ 1 Peter 5:10-11

Do you need comfort? You will find it here:
- ☐ Psalm 23
- ☐ Psalm 119:73-77
- ☐ Isaiah 12
- ☐ 2 Corinthians 1:3-7

Our Blessed Hope

When I was a young girl, my grandmother would sit in her rocking chair and dispense wisdom to me. "Child," she told me more times than I can count, "God didn't promise us smooth seas. But he did promise us a safe harbor." It didn't mean much to me back then, but it means a lot to me now. In life, there are good times and bad times, happy times and sad times, times of tumultuous storms and times of peaceful harbors. It's true for the non-Christian, and it's true for the Christian. It's true for those who are stricken, and it's true for their caregivers.

Back in the seventeenth century J. F. Starck wrote a prayer that has meant a lot to me. Perhaps it will be helpful to you too.

Lord! When I am in sorrow, I think on Thee.
Listen to the cry of my heart, and my sorrowful complaint.
Yet, O Father, I would not prescribe to Thee when and how Thy help should come.
I will willingly tarry for the hour which Thou thyself hast appointed for my relief.
Meanwhile, strengthen me by Thy Holy Spirit; strengthen my faith, my hope, my trust; give me patience and resolution to bear my trouble;
and let me at last behold the time when Thou wilt make me glad with Thy grace.
Ah, my Father! Never yet hast Thou forsaken Thy children.
Forsake not me.
Ever doest Thou give gladness unto the sorrowful.
O give it now unto me.

Always dost Thou relieve the wretched.
Relieve me too, when and where and how Thou wilt.
Unto Thy wisdom, love, and goodness, I leave it utterly.
Amen.

5

How Should I Pray?

IN THE BEGINNING I KNEW EXACTLY WHAT TO HOPE FOR, AND I KNEW HOW TO pray. When doctors told me, "Larry's just under too much stress," I made him comfortable and prayed for rest and peace for him. When they said he was showing symptoms of overwork, I made plans for a family trip and prayed for relaxation. When the diagnosis grew more serious—"a nerve disease," I was told, or "a psychiatric problem"—I asked for prayers on Larry's behalf, and I prayed for healing.

But as time went on, it became more difficult. How could it be that Larry had so many symptoms, and they were so varied, yet the doctors kept insisting those symptoms weren't connected? ("It's possible to have the flu and a broken arm at the same time," one doctor told me condescendingly.) In this day and age, when "modern medicine" and "miracle cure" call out from headlines and news reports, how could there be no answer to my husband's problems? No diagnosis? Not even an agreement that something really was wrong?

So, what did I hope? That I would find out something definite.

Maybe. Unless it was bad news. Then maybe not.

My prayers were also becoming more fuzzy. "God, please make it all right," I cried out in exasperation. "Please just let it be like it used to be."

One more neurologist, we were told. Exhausted and discouraged, with Larry arguing and protesting all the way, I reluctantly agreed to take him to one last doctor—Dr. Mark Corazza. After examining Larry, he said the most amazing thing: "There is something wrong, and we will work on it until we find out what it is."

Yes! Now I could pray a prayer of thanksgiving—I hoped. I could certainly pray for wisdom and guidance for the doctor and for anyone he decided to consult. I could also pray for a quick diagnosis, one with an easy—and not too expensive—cure. (Money was running low by then.) I could pray that this whole nightmare would soon be over.

When Dr. Collins from UCLA called with the diagnosis, "chorea acanthocytosis," he gave me a thumbnail sketch of the disease. Not good. Dr. Corazza gave me a more in-depth description of what to expect. Even worse. I searched out and read all the articles I could find on the rare and mostly unknown disease. Terrible! Now my prayer was that the doctors were wrong. That it *was* just stress. Or overwork. Or even a psychological problem.

When the signs became too obvious to deny, my prayer changed. Now it was "Dear God, If you will only heal him, I'll ..."

Hope, Prayers and Reality

How incomprehensible is the human mind. It represents all that is impenetrable about people. Larry, formerly a business administrator at a major national defense company, continued to change before my very eyes. The simplest checkbook calculations became impossible for him. He could no longer comprehend the monthly bills and bank statements we received. He could read, but he couldn't understand what he read. He could no longer tell left from right.

I prayed for comfort for him and for strength for me. I prayed for peace for him and for wisdom for me. I prayed for some sense of happiness for him and for endurance for me. I believe those prayers were answered. I did endure. And Larry, in his own reconfigured brain, did achieve a certain kind of happiness and peace.

For the One Afflicted

- *Pray for encouragement.* How lonely and frustrating and hopeless it must be from his point of view! How discouraged he must become! Pray for God's peace that passes understanding, for the grace God gives in direct proportion to the heaviness of the burden.

- *Pray that she will continue to value herself.* When injury or disease strikes a person, it is easy for her to fall into the pit of feeling worthless. Even if she is too sick or disabled to do anything—perhaps even to pray—ask God to let her know she is of immeasurable value simply because she *is*.

- *Pray that he will have the will to do what he can do.* Pray for the wisdom to encourage him without driving him. Pray that God will grant him an inner strength that can come only from above.

- *Pray that she will have a purpose in life.* How hard it must be for her to accept her limitations! Pray that God will give you wisdom in helping your loved one set new goals. Pray that she will be able to take in the truth that the simplest of things can be the most enjoyable. Pray that you will faithfully acknowledge her achievements, no matter how small, and that you will honor her joys, no matter how insignificant they may appear.

- *Pray with him.* Even if you think he doesn't understand. Even if you are certain he doesn't care. If he objects, make it short. If he is willing to participate, encourage him to do so. Demonstrate to him that you are praying and that you will not stop.

Larry's life shrank until it consisted of little but the here and now as it personally affected him. His goals were small and concrete—to be able to continue to ride his bike, to have plenty of potato chips to eat, to have his "lucky" clothes hand washed and ready to wear, to be able to sleep whenever he wanted.

But reality diluted my hopes and even my prayers. I began making promises to God. I proposed deals and made bargains. It's so difficult to deal with raw, stark reality without losing hope. It's hard to continue to pray in faith yet remain open to the answers you don't want.

So How *Do* You Pray?

In faith, that's how. We know the answer we want, but we don't know the answer God has for us. We want to remain open to him, but we don't want his response to be that thing we dread.

And so we pray in faith.

Sometimes we concentrate on *praying* and neglect the *doing*. As you are faithfully praying, put your prayers into action. Be practical in your encouragement and expectations. Actively reassure your loved one. Value her and remind her of how much God values her. Don't do for her what she can do for herself. Help her to set new goals and praise her for her achievements.

Help your loved one move beyond her own small world. Talk to her about current events. Read out of the newspaper. Watch television together and talk about what you are watching. Be sure she has a clock and a calendar to help her stay aware of the time, date, appointments and daily routines. Keep her horizons as wide open as possible in all the facets of her life. It will keep her hope alive.

Help your loved one feel useful by giving her responsibility, particularly the kind she was used to. When Larry was no longer working and had a lot of time on his hands, he learned to do a bit of the cooking. Are there jobs the person in your care can do? Peel potatoes? Sew a hem? Dust the furniture? Keep financial records? Feed the cat?

When Larry showed little interest in doing anything, I told him he had to be responsible for one job, but that he could choose what that job would be. He chose washing the car. Long after he was able to do much else, Larry washed the car every week. He didn't always do it well, but he did it. It was his job, he had chosen it, and it gave him a sense of accomplishment.

The easy way is to allow the person to act fragile, incompetent and dependent. Don't fall into that trap. Refuse to patronize her. If your loved one is an adult, treat her as one. Avoid baby talk. Look the other way and allow her to do the jobs she finds difficult, such as buttoning her clothes, cutting her meat or feeding herself. The more you do for her, the less she will be able to do for herself, and before long you will find yourself doing everything.

"But that's cruel!" you may be saying.

No it isn't. It's loving. Of course you will be willing to help when necessary. But don't steal your loved one's independence by overpampering.

One more thing: consistently express your affection by touching. Squeeze her hand. Kiss her cheek. Pat her shoulders. Hug her. Your touch will speak volumes about your love, caring, intimacy and acceptance.

When you are helpless, you may well have more questions than you have answers. God may seem very far away. You may be tempted to give up hope. You may doubt God's loving care. And yet it is precisely at these moments, when you least feel like it, that you most need to pray. In the

For Yourself . . .

- *Pray for the ability to express your emotions honestly.* Look at the Psalms and see how the psalmist prayed his anger (Psalm 109), his distress (Psalm 102), his tears (Psalm 17), his despair (Psalm 22) and his depression (Psalm 42). Using the book of Psalms as a guide, you too can express your pain and fears and doubts in prayer.

- *Pray that God will be your ever-present comfort.* No matter how busy you are during the day, no matter how many people are around you, your loneliness can be difficult to face. Again, the psalmists did a wonderful job of writing prayers of comfort. I found great solace in praying psalms of comfort such as Psalms 11, 23, 46, 91, and so many more.

- *Pray that God will help you to be wise in taking care of yourself.* God loves you. Ask him to help you value yourself and to show you ways to be kind to yourself.

- *Pray that you will never succumb to the temptation to rely on yourself.* Since in so many areas you have to be the one in control, it's easy to begin believing you really *are* in control. You aren't. Ask God to keep you ever relying on Him.

- *Pray that you will never demand a perfect life.* We live in a fallen world. Life is never going to be ideal. Perfection won't happen until we get to heaven. Ask God for the grace to live well the life he has provided you.

- *Pray for your family.* As problems occur, lay them out before God. Ask him for wisdom and patience. Ask him to keep you aware that you and the person in your care are not the only ones who are affected.

- *Pray for joy.* Yes, joy! Again, look at how the psalmists expressed joy even in the most difficult of situations.

- *Pray together.* Encourage your family to join you in prayer. Include the afflicted person. Ask your friends to join with you. You will gain strength from one another. Ask for prayer from your church. If they have a prayer chain, ask that you and your loved one be included on it.

- *Pray alone.* Pray for the person for whom you are caring. Pray for your family. Pray for the doctors who are treating your loved one. Pray for yourself. It is from prayer that you will gain your strength.

midst of tough times and challenging situations lie the greatest opportunities for learning how great and thorough God's love really is.

My grandmother used to have a pillow that read *"All sunshine makes a desert."* Pretty good philosophy. We were never meant to spend all our lives in happiness and comfort. If we did, how would we ever learn to trust in God? How could we know how faithfully he meets our needs?

"But God doesn't seem to hear my prayers," you may say. "At least, he doesn't answer them."

Hear you? Yes, God certainly hears you. And he does answer your prayers, too—always! But he doesn't always give you the answer you want. Instead, he gives you the answer that is best.

Ask God to help you accept his loving wisdom. Thank him for it if you can. If you cannot, ask him to make you thankful. And continue to pray and hope.

What shall you pray for? Pray for faith. Pray for wisdom. And pray that now, at this time when you and your loved one need it so much, God will hold you both close to his heart.

6

Him Versus Me
Where Is the Balance?

LARRY HAD ALWAYS ENJOYED BIKE RIDING, BUT IT WAS EVEN MORE IMPORTANT TO him after he could no longer drive. It allowed him to maintain an important touch of independence. But there was a problem. It was dangerous. He injured his arm in one fall and chipped a tooth in another. Because he didn't feel pain, he considered such injuries a minor inconvenience.

One day Larry came into the house with blood dripping down his face and soaking into his shirt and pants. "I think I broke a tooth," he told me. Actually, he had broken eight teeth, and it took seventeen stitches to close the gash in his chin.

"Please," I pleaded on our way to the emergency room, "stop riding your bike! It is too dangerous."

"Why do you have to make such a big deal out of everything?" he asked. "Anyone can have an accident."

That accident required eight trips to the dentist and three to the doctor, and cost almost two thousand dollars. But I didn't take away his bike. Everything reasonable in me insisted it had to be done, yet he had so little left.

Repeatedly caregivers find themselves asking, "Where's the balance here? Where *is* the balance?"

More Question Than Answers

As your loved one becomes increasingly dependent, you will find yourself facing more and more difficult questions. . The first place to go for answers is to the loved one's doctor. That doctor is most familiar with the intricacies of her condition and therefore is the best one to evaluate the care she needs, the best way to work with her, and what she can and cannot do.

Let's look at four of caregivers' most commonly encountered "Where's the balance?" questions:

1. Should I push him, and, if so, how hard? When we first learned his diagnosis, I started pushing Larry as hard and relentlessly as I could. "After all," I reasoned, "if he doesn't try, it's all over. And if *I* don't make him try, who will?"

Through frustrating and exhausting battles of tug-of-war, I finally learned a great truism: *I could not make Larry do anything.* Not even something good for him. Not even something that could prolong his useful life.

For a long time I insisted that Larry attend church with me. I thought it would be a comfortable place for him, a place where he would be welcomed, loved and accepted. He went, but I had to constantly shush him to be quiet. He could not follow the sermon, so he fidgeted and made inappropriate and distracting noises. He insisted on standing with the congregation, even though he often fell down. One Sunday, after Larry stumbled and struggled through yet another service, my daughter asked, "Mom, why do you insist he go?"

"Because it's good for him," I said.

"No," she answered. "You don't take him for *him*. You take him for *you*."

The more I thought about it, the more I realized she was right. I was doing it for me. Larry wasn't able to sit quietly and enjoy the service, and people rarely said much to him. When we got back home I said to him, "Larry, you don't have to go church anymore." He said, "All right." From then on, I just took him when he wanted to go, and we left when he wanted to leave.

For Larry, it was better to take him to the zoo or the beach and let him see the wonders of creation. It was better to put on a tape of the good old hymns he had heard since childhood and let him doze with praises in his ears. It was better for me to read favorite passages out of the Bible to him. There are times when you may need to push your loved one to do things he doesn't want to do, sometimes things that are uncomfortable or even downright painful. But most often you are better off to deal with your loved one with a gentle hand. Listen to him. Hear his whispered pain and frustration. Pull him into activity that is meaningful to him. Help him to stay in touch with God. Let him draw from your strength, as together you draw from the Lord's.

2. How much should I do for her, and how much should I insist she do for herself? Make it a habit not to do for your loved one what she can do for herself. From the beginning Larry wanted me to take over everything for him. And I tried to do just that. It was another caregiver who pointed out the error of that approach.

"Forget the 'I'll do it because it's easier for me,' " Kathy, the mother of a quadriplegic son, told me. "It is easier for me to phone a prescription refill into the pharmacist, but Thad can learn to manage his own supplies and order as necessary. It's part of learning responsibility and maturity. I would be remiss not to give him the chance to accomplish something and feel proud and successful."

Help your loved one come to terms with her difficulties and disabilities. Encourage her to take responsibility for herself. Feel for her. Be there for her. But do not take control and further disable her.

3. How much should I play the role of parent, and to what extent is it acceptable for him to play child? That depends. Certainly a child, however disabled, should be treated as a child. The roles of mama and papa are natural, realistic roles. The parents' challenge is to give their child the opportunity to live as independently as possible.

For a teenager the balancing can be especially tricky. On the one hand, teens need to take more responsibility for their own care and treatment. Doing so increases their self-reliance and sense of independence. On the other hand, parents still need to monitor their teens' treatment to be sure it is having the greatest possible benefit. Because it can be very difficult for parents to look at this objectively—in fact, many times the two parents disagree over how much help is too much—and teens may have their own agendas, it is a good idea to get someone else involved in setting those boundaries. Ask your child's doctor for guidance or perhaps for a referral to a specialist.

But when the sufferer is an adult, playing mama or papa can be frustrating and confusing to everyone. I know. For the last several years of his life Larry called me "Mommy," and that's how I acted. He wanted me to play with him, comfort him and take care of him. To me, he sometimes seemed like a bratty child. He pouted, sullenly rebelled and plotted to "get even." He wanted me to be the authority, but he resented it when I was. Someone had to be in charge, and there was no one except me to do it, but I wasn't sure how to take charge without diminishing our husband-wife role. The more Larry saw me as "Mommy," the more childish he became. The more childish he became, the more it drew out the authoritarian mother in me. It was hard on both of us.

The fact is, regardless of how childish your adult loved one may seem or act, he is *not* a child. While you may not be able to treat him as a responsible (capable, rational) adult, keep in mind that, though he has disabilities, he still *is* an adult. Do your best to help make his life more manageable. Be aware of the things that upset him or throw him off kilter, such as stepping outside his usual routine, having too many people around or being unable to lie down and take a nap at his usual times. (Larry became especially agitated if he thought he wasn't going to have a meal on time.) Understand that events such as holidays, birthday celebrations and family get-togethers can be a special strain and can bring out the worst in your loved one (and likely in you as well). Keeping his life on an even keel and free of surprises will help protect him from the frustration and confusion that can bring out unacceptable behavior.

Lay out for your adult loved one the responsibilities each of you will carry (even if his is simply to listen to music for a half-hour without calling you). Respect and deal with him as an adult even while you are performing tasks more appropriate for a child.

If you have already established a mother-child sort of relationship, it may be difficult to make a change. Be patient but firm. Both of you will benefit.

4. How can I keep the person I'm caring for from making me feel guilty? It isn't easy. Just ask Anne.

Anne's mother, Louise, is especially adept at manipulation. Four years ago Louise moved in with Anne, her husband and their three teenagers. Immediately the seventy-six-year-old woman employed her well-honed tactics of manipulative helplessness and control through guilt.

Guilt trips can be very hard to handle. What to do? Here are some ideas that can help you:

- Be aware of the specific manipulative tactics your loved one uses.
- Be aware of those spots in yourself that are most vulnerable.
- Plan your response ahead of time. For instance, you might be able to remove yourself from the situation. Or you might impose consequences for the person's actions.
- Ask someone less emotionally involved to step in and mediate.

"She knows exactly what she's doing," Anne says in frustration. "She's done it all her life—first to her own mother, then to my father, now to me. The difference is, I refuse to wait on her, and she retaliates by deliberately doing things to annoy me."

Louise carries her radio everywhere, and she turns it up so loud that it is difficult for family members to carry on a conversation. She disrupts the household by turning on the television at inappropriate times. She moves her chair and settles it in the most inconvenient of places, forcing Anne to work around her. And, perhaps most frustrating of all, she uses any excuse to get out of her bath and often refuses to have her hair washed for weeks at a time.

"In our state, a person who is legally mentally competent can refuse any service offered by a visiting nurse or health care worker. If Mom doesn't want her hair washed, the aide can't force her. Sometimes Mom goes for weeks without a shampoo. It drives me nuts."

When Anne tries to enforce the "house rules" by which the other family members live, Louise plays her trump card: guilt-producing tears.

It's an effective tactic. Many caregivers cave in to their loved ones' crying and accusations:

"You don't love me."

"I thought it would be so nice living here with you!"

"I'm just useless and in the way."

"Soon I'll be dead, and you won't have to worry about me anymore."

"After all I've done for you, you treat me this way!"

Operating out of guilt doesn't do anyone any good. Do all you can to keep from getting into a position where you can be manipulated. It can be terribly difficult, but if you give in to tears and accusations, the person will continue using them to get to you. The challenge is to differentiate between tears of physical or emotional pain, and tears of manipulation. Act immediately on the tears that well up because of real problems but firmly resist tears designed to force you into unreasonable demands.

Stress comes with the caregiving territory. But the more stress you carry, the more quickly you will burn out. Here are some strategies that can help you ease the stress load:

- *Learn to live with less-than-perfect solutions.* For instance, Anne craves quiet when she gets home from work—no CD player, no radio, no television. Her mother wants all of them going all the time. The solution? Louise has a small radio she carries with her and plays softly, and the television is limited to certain hours.

- *Step back and take a hard look at your situation.* What do you need? Make a list of the things that would help you, then ask yourself how you can get them.

- *Hire in-home help.* It may be a housecleaner. It may be a neighbor who will watch over the person in your care for an hour a day. It may be a teenager who will run errands or watch your children. For me, it was Dolly who lived in our extra room and, in exchange for room and board, helped with Larry, especially when I had to be out of town on teaching trips. Be sure all helpers know just what you expect of them. Be free with instructions and suggestions, but also be free with your praise and gratitude.

Set Limits

For your own health, both physical and emotional, begin by setting limits on the time and emotional and physical effort you put into caring for that other person. It would be wonderful if there didn't need to be a limit, but as we have seen, that isn't reality.

Where do you draw that line? It's different for different people. It's also different at different times in your life and in the various stages of your loved one's condition. No one can tell you precisely how much care you should be giving, when you need to hire help, or when to press for more assistance from other family members or social services. That's something you, with the help of your doctor, will have to determine.

Wherever you draw that line, stick to it. If you can be nudged beyond it, you will be. Again and again and again. By circumstances, by your loved one and by yourself. In time you will surely grow to resent it.

If you feel it's wrong for *you* to draw that line, ask yourself why. And if not you, then who?

Best for *Us*

Instead of thinking him versus you, direct your thoughts to what's best for everyone—your loved one, yourself and the family.

Take your own particular situation, with all of its frustrations and demands and blessings, and lay it before the Lord. Ask for his wisdom. Pray over the decisions you have to make. One by one place each of them before him.

Make certain that you are providing an emotionally safe environment for both of you.

- *If you have perfectionist tendencies, let them go.* Give yourself permission to ease up on your loved one and on yourself.

- *Stop saying yes.* Everyone thinks they know what is best for you and your loved one, but you are the one who is living it. You don't owe anything to all the advice givers. Consider the specifics of your situation and your relationship, and say a kind but firm "no, thank you" to everyone and everything that tear you down.

- *Take others up on offers to fill in for you.* This is an important point to reemphasize here. Even if the person under your care objects to you being gone, it will be good for both of you to get a bit of space between you.

- Keep the limits of the person under your care in mind. You will do well to make them your limits, too. I finally learned to replace "This is too much for you, Larry," with "I'm tired. Let's rest awhile."

I prayed and prayed about Larry and his bike. The answer came in a most unexpected way. Jim, the doctor husband of a friend of mine, also enjoyed biking. He met weekly with a group of men who rode around the foothills, and one day he called to ask if he could take Larry along with him.

Larry went, and he loved it. Jim offered to take him every week.

Jim was honest with me. He told me straight out, "At some point Larry is likely to fall and injure himself. But if you are willing to accept the risk, I will take him as long as he can manage a bicycle."

For the next year and a half, Jim did. He would come every Saturday morning and pick up Larry and his bike. He would stay with Larry throughout the ride and treat him to coffee and a doughnut afterward. When Larry couldn't keep up with the others, Jim stayed behind with him. When Larry ran into him and knocked his bike over, Jim said, "That's all right," and got Larry up and going again. For that year and a half, those Saturday morning bike rides were the most important thing in Larry's life.

Where's the balance? Give it over to God and ask him to show you.

7

Platitudes, Rumors & Easy Answers

FROM THE BEGINNING LARRY DIDN'T WANT ANYONE TO KNOW THERE WAS ANYthing wrong with him. He didn't realize that from simply looking at him and listening to him speak, it was obvious. But since he and I made no explanation, people looked and whispered and guessed.

It was time to break the silence.

Soon after people became aware of Larry's diagnosis and of the gloomy prognosis, wise sages and theologians sprang up everywhere. Platitudes ("Behind every cloud there's a silver lining"), easy answers ("Trust God and everything will turn out all right"), rumors ("Humph! You know what it really is, don't you? AIDS!"), surefire cures ("I know this guy who has a cousin who sells a wonder drug that can cure anything") and unwanted advice ("If I were you, I would . . .").

If we aren't careful, it will drown out the good and loving and helpful words that also come our way.

Empty Phrases and One-Size-Fits-All Scripture
They tumble out like flowery words embroidered on sunny pillows:

"God helps those who help themselves."

"When the going gets tough, the tough get going."

Well, what if I *can't* help myself? And what if, no matter how tough I try to be, I cannot get going? Platitudes mean nothing when our purely human resources are so inadequate.

Scripture is a wonderful source of strength and comfort, but when it is lifted out of context and thrown in a hurting person's face, it can cause a special kind of pain.

"God never sends burdens greater than you can bear."

I heard that misquoted phrase again and again. And each time I wanted to scream back, "What do you know about what I can bear? What do you know?"

"Give thanks for all things."

The implication of this oft-quoted verse was that if I were really giving thanks for all things and looking at our family's sufferings in the light of God's word, it wouldn't seem like suffering at all.

Make a special effort to search beyond the simple and look for the true message of love and grace that is available to you in God's Word.

Practicing Medicine Without a License

I thought I would suffocate under the mound of "free" samples and "trial" bottles of herbal remedies, body cleansers, healing teas and food supplements we received—all of which, by the way, were wonderworkers that just happened to be for sale. "Sure it's expensive," one friend counseled me, "but isn't your husband's health worth any price?"

It was a neurosurgeon in our church who finally took me aside and said, "This condition is not going to be helped by any mixture. You have a good doctor. Listen to him and don't waste a penny of your money on any more miracle cures. And don't let anyone make you feel guilty about it!"

Many times over I have thanked God for that perfectly timed word of professional advice.

But What Do You Say?

I am sure that when people spoke, they thought they were being helpful. But that's not how it felt to me.

"You're so brave," they said. I felt: *I'm so scared!*

"You're so strong," they told me. I felt: *I am really so weak!*

"You're an extraordinary person," they exclaimed. I felt: *So why do I feel like such a failure?*

"I don't know how you do it," they insisted. I felt: *I'm not at all sure I can make it through one more day.*

"We all look up to you," they told me. I felt: *Please, please! Don't lay that burden on me!*

All those "encouraging words" stung me like fire. I know people wanted to be constructive, but their words robbed me of the right to be weak and scared, and to cry freely. What I longed for was someone who would just sit and cry with me. Someone who would let me be helpless and afraid. Someone who wouldn't expect me to be a good example of anything.

When they say, "I know how you feel," you may want to shoot back, "Oh no you don't!" Instead say:

• "Thank you for caring."

• "We appreciate your prayers."

• "Some days are better than others. Perhaps tomorrow will be a better day."

• "What I really need is someone who will just listen."

"They mean well." That's what others tell us, and that's what we tell ourselves. Unfortunately, meaning well is not the same as speaking well. Whatever their intentions, some people just can't feel our pain. Even more fear it. Many simply talk on because they don't know what to say. In their stumbling around to say something, sometimes their theology slips.

God did not promise that his children would be lifted above all the troubles of this fallen world. Nor did he promise that those troubles would not cause us pain. In fact, God promised just the opposite—that we can expect our share of troubles. God "sends rain on the righteous and the unrighteous," Matthew tells us in his Gospel (5:45).

"But doesn't God help me?" you may be crying out.

Yes, of course he does. But he may not do it your way—or in a way you like, or even in a way you recognize. And he probably won't do it according to your timing either. God's ways are beyond our comprehension, and his timing is beyond our understanding. Whether or not he heals, whether or not he restores, one thing is certain: God's grace is sufficient for your needs, for his power is made perfect in weakness (see 2 Corinthians 12:9).

Other people may not understand that you are not helped by their insights and advice. They can't grasp how painful it is for you to see them smiling and praising, full of answers and speaking in a trivializing way of God's joy and peace while your heart is breaking. But lovingly, and believing that their intentions are the best, you can tell them so.

"Treat My Loved One with Dignity"
"My brother has cerebral palsy and is confined to a wheelchair," Jessie says. "I hate the ignorance and indignity with which he is treated. People stare at him, step away to avoid him, even pull their children back as though he has some contagious disease. It hurts me so to see perfectly intelligent people treat him like that. How must it make him feel? Don't all people deserve to be treated with dignity and respect?"

Yes they do. And as kindly as possible, you can say so. Don't say it when you are angry or upset; you may end up speaking more harshly than you intend. Do your best to let others know that even though your loved one has physical, mental or emotional challenges, he is a human being created in God's image, and he needs and deserves to be treated in a dignified, respectful manner.

"Thank You for Caring"
Give people the benefit of the doubt. Most think they are helping. They don't know what else to do or say.

"Please, It Is in God's Hands"
Probably the hardest things to hear are those that question your faith. "If you were really praying, God would have answered you by now," one man told me. Another person said, "When you learn the lessons God has for you, he won't have to keep trying to teach you."

Don't listen to recriminations that pull you down spiritually. Look to the Bible for the truth. The truth is that God chose not to heal even the apostle Paul. Although God is certainly able to heal any and all, he is under no obligation to heal anyone.

If healing is not in his will, what is?

Grace. That grace that grows greater to meet your greater need. That grace that is sufficient for you. That grace that allows his power to be made perfect in your weakness.

That's it! Within your weakness is a new fountain of grace. You may be frustrated and exhausted and sad and lonely. You may be disillusioned and discouraged. But underneath is a foundation of supernatural peace and strength.

If you are despairing that God has given you more than you can bear, you are right. But ask God to change your despair to hope. Trust him to bear all.

"If You Would Like to Help, I Have a List"

People often say, "Call if you need anything." Most of those offers are made in true sincerity, yet few of us ever call.

Think of what others can do to help your loved one and you. Write those things down in a list. Then when someone indicates a desire to help, you can say, "As a matter of fact, you can." Show the person your list and let him or her choose something to do.

Add to your list as other ideas come to your mind. Customize it to best suit you and your loved one.

There are many things that a concerned friend can do to help. Here are some ideas that will get your list started:

- Do shopping for you.
- Sit with your loved one so you can go out for a while.
- Bring a casserole or dessert in a disposable container. (Be sure to mention any diet restrictions.)
- Write thank you notes for you.
- Bring a magazine or newspaper to read to your loved one.
- Help with the housecleaning.
- Wash the car.
- Do some gardening or yard work.
- Bring a pet to visit.
- Play a game or work a crossword puzzle with the one in your care.
- Take your children for an afternoon.
- Include your kids in their family outing.

Shapes of Grace

There are people—sometime the most unlikely of folks—who come forward with love, caring support and earnest prayers that keep us going through our darkest hours. What treasures those people are! They help us learn to rest on the character of God. They encourage us to trust that all suffering takes place within his gracious sovereignty.

I know you can't understand why this is happening to your loved one and to you. Neither can I understand. And neither does that person who is stumbling along trying to give you words of comfort and encouragement. Suffering cannot be understood in purely human terms.

Ultimately it's not what people say, nor even what happens to us or our loved ones, that determines whether or not God is glorified in our individual lives. It is how we respond to what happens. When God's footprints are invisible to us, we can do nothing but trust that he is indeed by our side.

Toni, during her years of caring for her mother who was suffering from Alzheimer's disease, said, "I clung to God's promise: I will never leave you or forsake you. I prayed that God would walk with me and help me. And he did. But he never forgot Mama either. He stayed with her and helped her even when she was unable to ask him because she had forgotten how to talk."

And Toni learned something else too. "Like Habakkuk, I learned to take my post and to watch to see how God would work things out. And he did. Many times I wanted to climb up and help him, but he didn't need my help. Nor did he want it. I finally got the message that he can accomplish so much without my counsel and advice."

And sometimes in spite of the counsel and advice of other people, by the way.

The time will come when you will be able to sing, "I've learned to trust in God." And from what you've learned, you will be able to strengthen and encourage other caregivers who come along behind you.

8

The Forgotten
Caregiver

JOAN, SEVENTY-SIX YEARS OLD AND THE SOLE CAREGIVER FOR HER SERIOUSLY disabled husband, sat serenely as our support group chattered around her. One member's question—"What am I going to do when I can no longer keep up with this constant pressure?"—had opened up a sensitive subject close to all of us. Only Joan seemed unconcerned.

Finally one member addressed her personally. "How about you, Joan? Aren't you worried that the time may come when you just can't handle it anymore?"

Evenly and unemotionally Joan answered, "No. I've thought it all out. I bought a stepladder and a rope. I went to the library and got a book that showed me how to tie a noose. I hung the rope over a beam in the garage, and I put the stepladder under it. When it gets too much for me, I have my ladder and rope all ready."

We were shocked into silence. Caregiving was difficult, but each of us in the group was convinced it was worth it. That's why we were there. Since it was not a Christian group—it was run by the local Rehabilitation

Institute—and the leader was decidedly non-Christian in her orientation, the hope we Christians cling to wasn't particularly welcome. That made Joan's despair especially tragic.

In Hot Water

Joan's words nagged at me. How often I dropped into bed in the wee hours of the morning aching with exhaustion. Larry would awaken at first light. As soon as I heard him stirring, I'd drag myself up, still weary. Each morning I'd cry out, "I can't make it through today. I simply cannot!" When I fell into bed at night, I'd tell myself, *I did it! I actually made it through another day. But tomorrow . . . I'm not sure I can make it through tomorrow.*

Sometimes the endlessness was overwhelming. The constancy was suffocating. How long could I go on clinging by my fingernails? It seemed that nothing would ever change.

Caregivers can feel like the poor old frog I heard about in my high school biology class. Put him in a pan of cool water, and he'd sit there. Put the pan on the stove, and he'd sit there. Turn the heat on, and he'd sit there. The water would get hotter and hotter, and still he would sit. No need to put a lid on the pan; that old frog wouldn't jump out. The water would get hotter and hotter until he literally cooked to death without ever once trying to escape.

Look at what a woman who called herself "Loretta in Michigan" wrote to syndicated advice columnist Ann Landers:

> My husband has been diagnosed as having senior dementia. Two years ago, I had to leave a job I enjoyed to stay home and care for him. My problem is that I can't get out of the house and I feel myself stagnating.
>
> I have tried in subtle ways to tell my five children that I need a break to go shopping, visit the library, see a movie, or just take a drive to town. I don't expect them to take care of their father for any length of time, I just want them to take him out once in a while and leave me some time alone. . . .
>
> I tried to get my husband interested in the senior center, which is quite nice, but he refused to stay there without me. Lately, I've become impatient with him, and I'm ashamed of myself. If each of my children would take their father out just one day a month, it would help me enormously.

Loretta is a forgotten caregiver who needs help.

We all need a break now and then. We all have times when we feel overwhelmed. But here are some warning signs that the water is getting too hot:

1. No matter what you do, it isn't enough.

2. You have no time or place to be alone.

3. You feel uncomfortable about going away, even for a few hours or a day.

4. You feel there isn't anyone around to help.

5. Your family is getting impatient with you. They don't understand how hard it is.

6. You are missing work, and much of the time you are there you spend worrying.

7. You think it would be selfish to think of yourself.

8. You are feeling terribly sad, lonely or anxious.

9. You're tired most of the time and dread getting up in the morning.

10. You find yourself getting angry at the person you're caring for.

11. You're feeling over-stretched economically, emotionally or physically (or all three!).

12. You feel you're the only person in the world going through this.

13. Your family relationships are breaking down because of the caregiving pressures.

14. Caregiving allows you little time or opportunity for a social life.

15. You're going on in a no-win situation because you're convinced you have no options.

16. You're all alone and doing it all because you've turned down everyone who has offered to help.

17. Your coping methods have become destructive. (You're overeating or undereating, you're abusing drugs or alcohol, or you're taking your frustration out on your loved one.)

18. There are no more happy times. Loving and caring have given way to exhaustion and resentment.

But I Don't Want to Be Selfish

Of course you don't want to be selfish, and you don't want to look selfish. You don't want to resent everyone's concern and sympathy for your loved one while you remain the unnoticed one struggling to keep life going.

You don't want to begrudge that person all those cards and flowers and telephone calls of concern and sympathy. Still you can't help but feel that somewhere along the way you seem to have gotten lost and forgotten. Your life is anything but normal, yet you don't dare show weakness.

I worried aloud, "What if I break my arm and can't write? How will I support us?" My unspoken question was: *Who will take care of me?*

This is not a totally unfounded concern. Family and friends—and sometimes even health care professionals—often fail to realize that caregiving exacts a steep price from the person giving the care.

The Water Simmers

"My mom insisted she was not overdoing it or under too much stress," Paula said. "We all knew she had to be. Dad was always difficult, but after his stroke, he became a tyrant, demanding all her time and attention. She was sixty-three and still working part-time. Mom was always going a hundred miles an hour. She insisted she couldn't slow down. Then one night, sometime after she went to bed after midnight and before Dad started yelling for her at 6 a.m., Mom's heart stopped. No warning—nothing. She died in her sleep."

Even as the water around them simmers, many caregivers, like Paula's mother, insist they have to do it all. The cruel fact of the matter is that none of us—neither you nor I—is indispensable. Some of us have trouble accepting that. We have geared our lives around believing *If I don't do it, it won't get done—or at least it won't get done right!* Those can be killer beliefs.

Studies at Ohio State University suggest that the caregivers of people suffering from Alzheimer's disease are more likely to suffer depression than the general population, and their immune systems are less equipped to fight off illnesses like the flu. These findings will surprise few caregivers.

But I Feel So Guilty

You do feel guilty, and so did I. But you need to get over it. You have a responsibility to keep yourself healthy and to have a life of your own. If you don't, your loved one may suddenly be without your help.

But No One Else Does It Right

Are you sure about that? You may sincerely believe no one else is capable, but you are hardly in a position to step aside emotionally and be objective. It may be that you don't even have the necessary skills to be the best and only provider for your loved one. You can both benefit from getting some time and space between you. And think of it this way: by locking out other caring people, you are robbing them of the blessing they would receive by ministering to you and your loved one.

But God Called Me to This

God calls us to care and serve and be faithful, but he doesn't call us to kill ourselves. We are not being good stewards unless we are aware of our limitations. We need to know what and how much we can and cannot offer to give to someone who is suffering. Each of us has a limit. That limit depends on many things, including our other responsibilities, our personalities, our relationships with the ones who need our care, our own health and any number of other circumstances of our lives.

But I Have to Be There for My Loved One

Yes you do need to be there, and it's laudable that you see that. But please understand that no one—not even you—can be there for another person 100 percent of the time. To attempt to do so buys into the faulty illusion that you are infinite in your resources. The truth is that no matter how much you care, you are not superhuman. Like all of us you need balance in your life. You are not a failure if you don't do it all yourself.

Ask for Help

If you are like most caregivers, you started out saying "thanks, but no" when people offered assistance. You didn't want to impose. You wanted to show that you were strong and independent. And you honestly thought you could manage alone. Now things are starting to pile up, and you're feeling stressed. But it's awkward and humbling to go back and admit that, yes, you do need help after all.

I tried very hard to keep our shattered life as normal as possible. But Larry's condition worsened, I had a mounting pile of paperwork to deal with, I had writing work to do without the necessary tools (no computer!), and there were endless decisions to make about rebuilding the house. Also, my daughter announced her engagement—we had a wedding to plan! To top it off, our church was going through a major problem that was threatening to split it in two, and I felt terribly pressured and torn about that. By the time I realized I needed help, I realized that I had needed it months earlier!

Seeking help is a sign of strength. But where do you find it?

Find It in Your Family

Start by reaching out to your extended family. Find out when and how you can get together—in person, by telephone, through e-mail or letters—to talk about what others can do to help. One person may be able to contribute time. ("I will take charge of all the paperwork.") Another may want to help financially. ("I will pay for her medications.") Another may be able to be on call. ("If you ever have to get away for the afternoon, I'll come over.") Yet another may offer to help out emotionally. ("I'll call every Sunday to talk to her and also to see how you are doing.") There will probably also be those who will insist that they can do nothing or, even worse, who promise to help but will never be available, but you will likely find that the majority will be truly cooperative and helpful.

Depending on the condition of the person in your care, another family member may be able to get your loved one to do things you cannot. As Larry's illness progressed, he increasingly saw me as the enemy and everyone else as lined up either on his side or on mine. He trusted only the ones on his side. Since his father was the one he trusted the most, whenever I needed Larry's cooperation, I enlisted his father's help. Cliff was a lifesaver.

Give your family an opportunity to be involved. It will be good for all of you.

Find It Among Your Friends

A rich and wonderful source of assistance and support, some friends will be willing to help you on a regular basis, while you will find others more spontaneous in their assistance.

My neighbor Jan called one morning and said, "I just read a letter to Ann Landers in the newspaper. It said, 'Don't put off helping another person. The right time is now.' So I'm calling to see if I can come over today to stay with Larry so you can go out to lunch and do some shopping." She came over, her arms filled with games to play, and told me to take my time. Feeling guilty, I was back home in less than two hours. When she found out I had spent my time away buying groceries and running errands, she said, "But I wanted you to have fun! I'll come back tomorrow. Call a friend and have lunch, and stay out all afternoon!" I did, and it was great.

Jan came back many afternoons to sit with Larry. Sometimes I went out, and sometimes I just locked myself in the bathroom and soaked in a warm tub of bubbles and snoozed. Either way it was wonderful.

Do friends volunteer to help you clean? Garden? Baby-sit with your little ones? Return telephone calls for you? Write thank you notes? Take them up on their offers.

Find It in Your Church

For several years Don, an acquaintance from church, came over every week to read to Larry. Neither Larry nor I had known him well, and I was really impressed by his faithfulness. One day I asked, "Don, why are you so good to Larry and me?"

"Because," he said, "I am doing it as unto the Lord."

After years in a large church in which Larry, our children and I had all been very active, I moved to a tiny congregation that was in the process of planting a church. What a wonderfully supportive group of people it was! They helped me emotionally, physically and spiritually. And they showed a great love and compassion for Larry.

Give your church family a chance to put feet to their faith by ministering to your physical family. If they help on a rotating basis, it won't be too large a commitment for any one person.

Find It Among Health Care Professionals

Whereas family and friends can help you physically and emotionally, health care professionals can assist in other ways. Ask your loved one's doctor to suggest agencies or professionals that can lighten your load. Dr. Corazza recommended the Rehabilitation Institute. The social worker there helped Larry and me set realistic expectations. Dr. Corazza recommended Work Inc., a sheltered workshop that allowed Larry to continue working for almost two years. This job did wonders for his self-esteem, allowed him some sense of independence and allowed me time to do the things I needed to do.

Also, health care professionals provide an air of authority that we care-givers sometimes lack. When I knew that my husband had no business driving a car, I enlisted the help of both his doctor and the psychologist who was working with Larry. They accomplished what I couldn't.

Look for Other Resources
There are resources available. Make it a priority to acquaint yourself with them.

- *Learn all you can about your loved one's condition.* Check the public library. If there is a medical library nearby, see what's available there. And don't forget the Internet. A librarian, friend, or son or daughter can help you look if you are unfamiliar with its use. I even found chorea acanthocytosis on it!

- *Look for a support group.* It could be a real help to you and maybe to other members of your family as well.

- *Ask your church for referrals.* Your pastor or priest may be able to steer you toward a Christian counselor or support group, or to other resources that will encourage your faith.

- *Ask your doctor or other health care professionals.* They are in touch with organizations, resources and options that the rest of us are not familiar with.

- *Look in your telephone book.* In addition to the name of the condition from which your loved one is suffering, check under such headings as *Senior Care, Mental Health, Rehabilitation* or *Respite Care.*

- *Call your local social services department.* You can find the number in the telephone book. Ask them for suggestions for services that would be appropriate for your specific circumstances.

Respite Time
Pace yourself and schedule breaks during the day. You need time to get away. Give yourself a chance to sit down. Set aside a bit of time to stretch out and read something you enjoy. Listen to music or a favorite radio program. Play a tape or CD you especially like.

Many community services offer respite for caregivers. If you need information about services in your community, or if you need help exploring respite options, call Family Caregiver Alliance at (800) 445-8106. Ask to speak to a resource specialist.

Here are some ideas on how you can get respite time:

- Check into hiring someone from a home health care facility to come in several hours a day or week.
- Hire a student nurse to help out occasionally.
- If several family members are involved in the care, set up a schedule for routine tasks.
- Check into the availability of a daycare facility. Ask about special requirements. Some, for instance, have an age limit or require that the person be ambulatory. Some only serve people suffering from a specific disorder. Many facilities are concerned with such general areas as nutrition, recreation, physical well-being, safety and rehabilitation.
- Some home social services are available at reduced rates through government assistance. These include home health care, visiting nurses, respite care, daycare and meal-assistance programs. Do some telephoning and check them out.

Take Care of Yourself Physically

Professionals tell us that sleep is the most common unmet need of caregivers. Even though there don't seem to be enough hours in the day, it's vital that you get the rest and exercise you need. "I can prescribe pills for you," one doctor told me, "but the best prescription is sleep and physical activity." One of the places we lived while our house was being rebuilt was a condominium with a swimming pool, and I swam laps every day. The more frustrated and discouraged I was, the more laps I swam. I referred to my worst days as "forty-five lap days"!

Swimming may not be your thing. Just think of some fitness routine that appeals to your interests and can be squeezed into your schedule, then stick with it.

As for rest, do your best to stay away from sedatives. The best techniques for promoting good, healthy sleep patterns are relaxation (try reading, listening to music, taking a warm bath), deep breathing, more vigorous exercise or any other activity that helps to clear your cluttered mind.

Handling Stress

Don't underestimate the effects of stress. Your body reacts to it as if you were trying to escape from danger. Your pulse quickens, your blood pressure goes up, your immune system slows down, your stomach increases its production of acid, and your muscles tense as if they were getting ready for action. These physical responses were deeply imbedded in early humans to protect them from marauding beasts and physical attacks. Since your body can't tell the difference between physical attack and emotional attack, the results are the same.

But as psychologist James E. Loehr writes in *Stress for Success:* "It's not stress that's the issue; it's insufficient intermittent recovery." Trouble comes when the stress is unrelenting. It makes you more susceptible to illness, and it makes your recovery slower. Little wonder a recent study showed that it took nine days longer for constantly stressed family caregivers to heal from wounds than it took other people of the same age.

If you are to stay well and remain able to give care, you *must* control the stress. And there are only three ways to do it:

1. Reduce the factors that cause your stress.
2. Improve your ability to cope with the stress that remains.
3. Share your stress with someone who can help you handle your stressful problems.

We all differ in our ability to handle stress. Some are good at letting it roll off; others let it churn and boil inside. Come to know your tolerance.

"I wish my mom had known her limits," Paula says. "I wish the rest of us had seen the signs of overstress in her and had warned her to heed them. But we didn't, and now I'm the caregiver, and I am determined not to make the same mistakes."

So what does Paula plan to do differently? "I love my father, but I accept that I have limits," she says. "I'm getting help from the very beginning. I resolve not to follow my mother, roaring along at full speed as if nothing will ever happen to me. If it happened to her, it can happen to anyone."

So what are your signs of overstress? Do you get irritable? Angry? Depressed? Anxious? Unable to sleep? Learn to recognize the signs in yourself, but also pay attention to others who warn you of signs that concern them. They may be more objective than you are. When in doubt, see a doctor or other professional who can help you determine when stress is reaching a danger point.

Have an Activity List

Think some more about your time away. To make the most of it, ask yourself these questions:

- ☐ What things would I really like to do?
- ☐ What time can I make for doing these things?
- ☐ What can I adjust to make time for these things?
- ☐ Who can I get to help me?
- ☐ With whom can I do some of the things I enjoy?

Stay involved in the activities you already do, or get reinvolved in those you have enjoyed in the past. Also be open to exploring new activities.

Need activity suggestions? Here are a few:

- an exercise class
- movies or plays
- a support group
- shopping outings
- a favorite park or beach
- the zoo
- lunch with a friend
- club meetings
- Bible study
- museums
- a walk with friends

Build on Your Faith in God

In the pressure of time, and with demands coming from all sides, it is easy to skip spending time with the Lord. A quick on-the-run prayer of "Help me!" isn't enough to keep you spiritually nurtured. It is important to be in fellowship with a group of Bible-believing Christians. It's vital that you read God's Word for instruction and encouragement. It is essential that you pray, laying your concerns and fears and pressures before the Lord and asking for his guidance and direction.

Does your church have a prayer chain? Ask to be included in it. It will keep others informed of your family's needs and challenges so they can pray specifically. Is there someone who has offered to be diligent in prayer for you on an ongoing basis? Take that person up on it. Many people say, "I'll pray for you," but there are a few who really, consistently will. Gerda was a friend I could always depend on. And because her prayers were always there, so was she.

The Water Starts to Boil

Stress and pressure have a way of sneaking up on us. Before we realize it, the water starts to boil. If you recognize these signs, you are pushing it too far:

☐ You are exhausted, but you cannot sleep.

☐ There is such a change in your appetite that you are losing or gaining a substantial amount of weight.

☐ You are using more, or depending on, sleeping pills or other medications, alcohol or caffeine.

☐ You are neglecting your physical needs.

☐ You are increasingly irritable and short-tempered.

☐ You find it difficult to concentrate and pay attention.

☐ You are extremely tired and have little energy.

☐ You have gotten rougher in your handling of the person in your care. You may even have struck out at him.

☐ You are plagued by nightmares.

☐ You have recurrent thoughts of death or suicide.

If you recognize any of these signs, see a counselor who will listen and not judge, who will guide but not moralize. Ask your physician for a referral.

No one can tell you how to cope with your caregiving situation. It is something you will have to learn for yourself by trial and error. But the starting point is to accept that you have limits.

By taking care of yourself you not only extend your capacity to give care without burning out, you also allow yourself to grow in faith and in maturity.

9

Someone to Lean On

I REMEMBER IT CLEARLY AND ALWAYS WITH MORE THAN A BIT OF HUMILIATION. I was at a Christmas party. There were a lot of people I knew there—some were very good friends. In fact, I hadn't wanted to go. I was so emotionally exhausted I could hardly talk without crying. That very morning I had gone to the grocery store, and when I couldn't find the brand of chicken chili that was on sale, I stood blubbering helplessly in front of a perplexed boxboy.

But I did go to the party, and it was actually a nice diversion. Near the end of the evening, a woman named Nancy, whom I hardly knew at all, made some friendly comment about the cool weather and how nice the fire in the fireplace felt. Then she made the mistake of casually asking, "So, how are you?" and I started to talk. Poor woman! I could see her eyes darting around, looking for a way of escape. But I wasn't about to give her one. I *needed* to talk. I can remember purposely taking a breath in the middle of each sentence because I knew if I paused even briefly at the end of one, she would quickly excuse herself, and I would be left alone by the fire. So I talked and I talked and I talked and I talked. I told her my whole history and Larry's too, and how hard and confusing life was, and how I didn't know what I was going to do.

I left the party feeling better. Nancy, I'm certain, left hoping our paths would never cross again.

It's hard to stand alone. Relatives and friends care, but they have their own lives to live. Those around you get tired of hearing the same thing over and over again, yet you have a consuming desperation to tell it over and over again.

There Are the Kids

Like you, your children are personally involved in and affected by the caregiving situation. So are they good confidantes?

Absolutely not.

If you are caring for a spouse, the temptation is to embrace your child as a replacement for your partner. It's destructive to confide in your child as you would in an adult partner, or to look to your young person as a comforter or a sounding board for your needs.

You should talk to your children and encourage them to talk to you. Just don't lay the burden on them.

Who, then, can you lean on?

Certainly your friends and family want to be there for you. And you need them to. But it is important that you not wear them out. Here are some suggestions for finding an appropriate person to lean on.

Others Who Have Been There

People who have walked this path before you have a great deal to offer, both in insight and in understanding. They likely know more about your needs than you do, and they understand how important a listening ear is. Once your caregiving situation becomes known, you will likely have those who will come to you and say, "I spent time doing exactly what you're doing. I would love to share with you some of the things I learned." Take them up on the offer. An older woman from church took me to lunch and told me about her caregiving years with her father. I poured my soul out to her for two hours. She sat and listened, nodded her head in understanding, squeezed my hand and shared her wisdom. It meant so much to me.

What if no one offers? Then you take the initiative. Look for someone of the same sex who has been a caregiver and ask if you can talk. If the person responds less than enthusiastically, look for someone else. Pray that God will lead you to the right person.

A Professional Counselor

Talking to a professional counselor can be a great help. It may or may not be an ongoing process; just a session or two might be all you need. Professional counselors let you talk and help you explore your options; that's what they are paid to do. They also ask probing questions that help you to gain insight and to feel less helpless. While there are many good and effective counselors who are not Christians, one who is coming from the same orientation you are will be able to better understand and work within your Christian frame of reference. Certainly it is best to work with someone who accepts God's Word as the authority. However, if such a person is not available, or if for some reason the one who is available is not appropriate for you, look for someone who will respect and work within your beliefs. (One counselor told me to "dump the guy." I didn't go back to her!)

Actually it was my dentist who first suggested I see a counselor. I went to see him about a painful jaw that I was certain meant that I needed a dreaded root canal. Imagine my surprise when he told me, "The problem is that you're clenching your jaw and grinding your teeth—grinding them so hard, in fact, that two teeth are seriously worn down. My advice is to get someone to help you deal with your stress."

I found a good marriage, family and child counselor (MFCC) who not only was a Christian but also specialized in working with people who had a family member with brain illness or damage. I spent many hours pouring out my heart and hurts to him. My first breakthrough was getting to where I could make it through the hour without using up half a box of tissues. The counselor listened to me, made comments, at times helped me correct my thinking, and offered advice and direction. It was extremely helpful.

"But I can't afford that!" you may be saying. "Those guys charge a huge amount."

Before you rule it out, check your health insurance policy. Mine paid for my treatment for two entire years. Some therapists charge on a sliding scale so that the charge is adjusted to what you are able to pay. There are also free services available for those who meet the qualifications. Look up the telephone number for the social services office in your area and ask what options are open for someone in your specific situation.

A Special Person

Ask God to send you one special person who will be able and willing to walk with you through this time. My special person was Gerda. She listened to me endlessly. She had ideas and sometimes offered advice that I was free to accept or not. She comforted me, and she brought me tapioca pudding and chocolate ice cream because she knew they were comfort foods to me. She prayed with me regularly. She faithfully visited with Larry, and she helped out with him when it was beyond my strength to do so. She also kept me grounded in reality. What a gift from God Gerda was to me!

There Is Help

Talk individually to each person in your family. Let them all know you realize how much the caregiving has changed their lives. Encourage them to voice their fears and concerns.

"My mother lived with us while she was dying of cancer," one woman said. "It wasn't until many years later that I learned that my daughter was terrified that the rest of us were going to 'catch' it from her. To this day that lingering fear haunts my daughter."

Perhaps you are asking, "Shouldn't I just trust God with my family members?"

Of course you should. But trusting God doesn't mean you shouldn't take advantage of programs set up to assist families in pain. Don't be too embarrassed or ashamed to get your child (or yourself, for that matter!) professional help.

Statistics indicate that caregiving families have extraordinarily high rates of stress and also of relationships pressured to the breaking point. In an effort to reach out to the needs of families, Joni and Friends (JAF, the ministry headed by quadriplegic Joni Eareckson Tada) provides a wonderful summer program at various locations around the country. With

Grief and stress in children can take on many different forms. You may notice:

- denial ("Problem? What problem?")
- indifference ("I don't really care.")
- regression ("I want to suck my thumb!")
- panic ("What are we going to do?")
- acting out ("You can't make me!")
- fear ("Will I catch the same thing? Does it run in our family?")
- guilt ("If something had to happen to someone in this family, it should have happened to me.")
- self-blame ("If only I hadn't been bad, Mommy wouldn't have been in that accident.")
- hopelessness ("Nothing will ever be right again.")
- physical changes ("I'm not hungry." "I can't sleep." "I'm always tired." "My stomach hurts.")

If any of these symptoms are severe or persistent, get help. If any of the following occur, don't wait for severe or persistent signs. Get help immediately if your child

- threatens suicide
- physically assaults others
- is cruel to animals
- behaves aggressively toward other family members
- becomes involved with drugs or alcohol
- begins to commit serious delinquent acts
- is unwilling or unable to get along with other children

---

activities for the entire family, everyone can relax, have fun and try new things. (To receive a brochure, see the address listed in appendix two.)

Keep your eyes open. Ask questions. Follow up on recommendations. You will find that help is all around.

Others Who Are Walking the Same Path

A woman came up to me in the grocery store one day and slipped me a scrap of paper with her name and telephone number on it, and the notation: *Huntington's Disease Support Group.* "Forgive me if I'm being too bold," she whispered, "but I couldn't help noticing your husband. This might be helpful to you."

I didn't know what to think. Larry didn't have Huntington's disease—although I later found out that his condition was much the same and is even often misdiagnosed as Huntington's. But why would I want to go to a support group anyway? Another meeting was all I needed!

Look and see what might be available for you. Here are some suggestions:

- Some employers offer employee assistance programs that include help for the entire family. (Ours did, and it was great.)

- Schools often offer counseling for children. This is especially helpful for adolescent and teenaged children, because they tend to have greater difficulties than younger ones.

- Look around you and see if there is a role-model type person who might be willing to spend time with your young person. (Your church is a great place to start your search.) Talking to and listening to someone other than Mom or Dad can make a big difference.

Yet I did have questions, and I did have concerns. For instance, I couldn't stop worrying: *What would Larry be like next year? In five years? In ten?* And I was haunted by fears: *If handling him is so hard now, how can I ever hope to cope with him when he gets worse?* So I decided to give the group a try.

I was impressed by the openness of the people there, and I was surprised by what I heard. Other people were experiencing the same things as I. They were feeling the same kind of anguish I was feeling. And there was more. People in the group talked about and shared ideas on ways to ease the physical and emotional drain of working with a family member with so devastating a condition.

A woman named Helen told me about a respite-care program at a local hospital one weekend a month. Larry could have an enjoyable time away while I got two and a half days off. A young man named William told me about a doctor at the University of California in Irvine who was doing research on diseases related to Huntington's who might have more information for me. He did.

Someone once described friendship as "a sharing of hearts." I like that. Something special happens when a group of vulnerable people shares their suffering hearts with one another. No one can understand and share your feelings, your fears and your tears like others who are walking the same road. And you will help them by hearing and sharing their feelings, fears and tears as well.

You can also share insights and resources. It is easier to accept suggestions from others personally acquainted with the particular difficulties of caregiving. They can be your best teachers and guides. They can lead the way to greater patience, compassion and faith. Through them you will experience the blessing of having sympathetic ears to hear you, but you will also learn the importance of moving outside of yourself and reaching out to other caregivers.

"But there is no support group here," you may be saying.

Perhaps you should consider starting one. It could be made up of caregivers from a variety of situations (for example, one might have a parent with Alzheimer's, another a child with cerebral palsy, another a spouse with multiple sclerosis).

How Can I Start a Support Group?

There are many ways of forming a group. The best? Whichever one works for you. Here are some guidelines that can help:

1. Tell your doctor, counselor and pastor of your desire to start a support group. Ask for suggestions and enlist their help.

2. Set a place, day and time for a first meeting. (It's a good idea to allow three or four weeks to prepare.)

3. Let your intentions be known.

☐ Write an announcement that can be read at church.

☐ Advertise in a local or area newsletter or newspaper.

☐ Use free radio or TV announcements such as local talk shows.

☐ Solicit cooperation from other churches.

4. Prepare a sign-in sheet to use at the first meeting. Ask for the following information:

☐ name, address, telephone number, fax number, e-mail address

☐ name of person for whom care is being provided

☐ condition from which the person suffers

☐ his or her current health status
☐ relationship with the person
☐ who else is in the household (children, spouse, parents)
☐ affected person's employment status

If yours is a Christian support group, make sure prayer is an important part of your time together. If it is not a Christian group, bathe it in prayer on your own or, even better, with other concerned Christians.

At the first meeting, let all present introduce themselves and briefly tell their situations. (It's best to have a time limit so that no one takes over.) Then

1. Explain the format of the meetings. (Speakers? Sharing of information? Prayer?)

2. Hand out a sheet of "rules" for your group. Include such essentials as

☐ *Confidentiality must be respected.* This is extremely important. Confidentiality builds trust. Stress that what is said in the group *must* remain in the group.

☐ *Don't judge one another.* When it's your turn to listen, listen patiently. When it's your turn to share, share openly. If there is a situation in which you truly need to call another to accountability, do so in love.

☐ *Each person is an expert in his or her own right.* Each can teach others, and each can learn from others.

☐ *The moderator has the last word.* He or she can keep one person from monopolizing the time, can draw in those who are more hesitant to speak, and can use judgment as to who needs extra time. (If at all possible, it is best to have a professional Christian counselor for this job.)

☐ *Be considerate in your treatment of others in the group.* Feelings are exactly that—feelings. They are not wrong or sinful. Don't criticize each other. Encourage one another to turn difficult emotions over to the Lord and pray together to that end.

☐ *Don't carry on "side" conversations.* The person who has the floor deserves everyone else's undivided attention.

☐ *Each person is responsible for his or her own actions.* We can grow by changing ourselves, but we cannot control others. We can react to their behavior, but we cannot change it. That doesn't mean we shouldn't point out scriptural teachings in regards to actions. We should. But understand that you cannot change that other person.

☐ *Each person will have the opportunity to share without interruption.* You might want to mention a time limit here, however.

3. If there is time, ask people to share a particular joy, sorrow or blessing in their lives.

4. Announce the place, day and time of the next two meetings and the programs you will have.

5. Dismiss promptly.

Is a Support Group Really Important?

You are busy, busy, busy. You have no time to yourself the way it is. So what is there in a support group that will make the extra commitment worth your time?

A support group will offer you

Empathy. You will see that you are not alone with your problems.

Acceptance. You will experience acceptance rather than judgment.

Education. You will get a clearer explanation and more realistic expectations from others who are at various places in the caregiving journey than from perhaps anywhere else.

Catharsis. You can find a release from your emotions through the experiences of others.

Hope. Through each other's situations, you will see that you, too, can deal with your problem.

Humor. You can laugh with them like you can laugh with no others.

Empowerment. Your group will help you see options you never imagined existed.

"I speak about myself," Paula said in her support group, "but in so many ways you are all like me. I gain understanding and strength from you. I don't have to explain and justify my feelings, wants, desires and fears. I just mention what I'm going through, and you all understand because you've been there too."

The Ultimate Support

As wonderful and important as others are, no person or support group can offer the support and comfort available from the Lord.

"Lo, I am with you always," Jesus promised.

He asks us to live by faith. That means walking without being able to see where the path is going. The unfathomable depth of God's purposes can sometimes be baffling and scary. But the reassuring fact is that God is in control. We are called to trust, though not necessarily to understand.

You and your entire situation are completely known to God, and you are completely loved by him. No matter how alone you may feel, he is right beside you—always. When the night looks the darkest, his right hand is holding you securely. He is always there for you to lean on, even in the times of greatest loss.

10

Dealing with Losses

POOR LARRY. THE LAST TEN YEARS OF HIS LIFE WERE MARKED BY A RELENTLESS series of losses. Some were physical (driving, doing woodwork, holding down a job). Others were emotional (taking pride in the achievements of his children, feeling productive, being interested in the world around him). Not only was the onslaught of loss after loss devastating to him, it also chipped away at his image of himself as a worthwhile person.

Like many afflicted adults Larry was determined to maintain control by hiding the signs of his failing health and his difficulties in coping. In the months before his symptoms became obvious, he had told me he was getting promotion after promotion at work. (The truth was that responsibility was being taken away from him as he became less able to perform.) He had complained about the reckless drivers in the parking lot at work who were constantly hitting his parked car. (I later found out that it was Larry who had been hitting other cars.) He had told me I was a nag who made him so nervous he knocked things over and dropped things. (His disease was causing him to be less and less coordinated.)

I'm sure that, at first, denial was his way of maintaining dignity and minimizing his losses, but in time he began to believe his own deceptions. Yet I was losing too. The husband I had known and loved had turned into my enemy, and I couldn't understand why. My house and everything we had accumulated in twenty years of marriage was gone due to fire. My children were two thousand miles away at college. My church was embroiled in bitterness and strife. My life was falling apart, and I could do nothing to stop it.

It was harder and harder for me to remember how it had once been: Larry and I together reading the Sunday newspaper, holding hands in church, sharing an order of hot onion rings, breathing in the brisk evening air around a campfire, finding the perfect Christmas tree for the cheapest price. As time went on and things grew harder, it became difficult for me to remember what it was in him that I had loved.

I was losing my connection with Larry. During dinner I groped for something to talk about. In the evening I folded clothes or ironed or worked on my writing while he dozed before the television. It seemed comforting and reassuring to him to have me in the same room so long as he had complete charge of the remote control. That was extremely important to him. He seemed gratified that he could still be in charge of something.

A Range of Losses

So many losses.

First Larry couldn't drive, later he couldn't ride his bike, finally he could barely walk. First he couldn't button the small buttons on his shirtsleeves, then he couldn't shave, then he couldn't shower alone.

Each loss required mourning. Yet I never saw Larry shed a tear. It was rare that he shared even a bit of his sense of loss. That caused me to believe he didn't feel it at all. I know now that wasn't so. But back then all I could feel was my own mourning over my own losses.

I think the worst loss of all was the loss of being two people who cared for and about each other. Gone were our shared interests. Gone were our dreams for the future. Gone were the stimulating conversations and thought-provoking discussions. Gone was my sense of security and safety.

Gone was the husband I had known and loved.

And yet how could I mourn? Larry was still there. He lived with me; we ate at the table together; we slept together; we rode in the car together. It was as if we were frozen in time. Larry was not dead, but neither was he a part of me.

This kind of loss leaves caregivers with unresolved grief mixed with a heavy dose of guilt and sprinkled liberally with anger.

Depending on the specifics of your loved one's disability, you may be struggling with one or more of these losses:

- independence
- security
- a sexual partner
- a confidante
- a best friend
- a parent
- hopes for what could have been
- expectations (especially for a child)
- part of yourself

Social Losses

As Larry's social skills continued to deteriorate, he developed more and more inappropriate behaviors. If he felt tired, he would curl up in a corner and go to sleep no matter where we were. He became obsessed with money, searching chairs and cushions for lost change, even stopping strangers to ask for money. And "magic," an idea that would have brought sneers from him before, began to rule his life: he had "lucky charms" hidden everywhere, and he would wear only his "magic" clothes, which he had to put on in a ritualistic way.

Then a new and upsetting symptom emerged. Larry began to babble obscenities and curses. Sometimes he would yell them out.

By this time almost everyone avoided us.

Eating was Larry's great joy, and he loved to go out for meals. For special treats I would take him to casual places on off-hours and request a booth in the back corner. One afternoon, as we were leaving a restaurant, a woman took me by the arm, pulled me aside and hissed, "Why do you bring him out in public?"

How I grieved for our lost social life!

Most caregivers experience a remarkable change in their social lives. Often the afflicted person isn't really in the mood to have friends over. Even when close friends or family members visit, the person may tire easily or become irritable.

It surely isn't like it used to be.

Loss of Empathy

When Charles was felled by a heart attack and then by a stroke that left him virtually helpless, his wife Andrea was heartbroken. "He was only fifty-three," she recalls, "and a handsome, dashing fifty-three at that."

Andrea nursed him lovingly. She quit her job so she could be at home with him full-time. With Charles unable to return to his high-profile executive position and with Andrea no longer working, she decided to sell their rambling family home of twenty-two years and buy a condominium.

It was while Andrea was packing up papers from Charles' study that she found the brown leather case with the love letters and receipts. At first she couldn't comprehend what she was reading. Then with a crushing blow it became clear to her: for more than five years Charles had been carrying on an affair with Stephanie, the best friend and former college roommate of their oldest daughter, Kelly. The things Andrea read in the letters curled her hair. Her Charles! Her soul mate! The father of her children! The chairman of the board of deacons in their church!

After a few telephone calls and a drive to an apartment ten miles away, Andrea knew more than she ever wanted to know. Stephanie, the "other woman," and Charles had set up housekeeping in a luxury apartment.

It explained a lot. Andrea never could understand why they had to take out a loan for their youngest son's college expenses. "It's the stock market," Charles had explained. "The money's there, it's just all tied up." The "new position" he had touted that entailed all those out-of-town trips? Stephanie. And the "start-up costs" for the proposed overseas branch? Stephanie. The weekend their middle child had surgery on her knee, and he couldn't be there because he was suddenly "called away on business"? Stephanie.

Caregiving is difficult when the person you are called to care for has been your loving parent, your dear child, your faithful spouse. So what is it when you are called to care for a parent who was selfish and unloving? A child who was rebellious and cruel? A cheating, unrepentant spouse?

What about when you are giving care to someone who doesn't seem to deserve your sacrifice?

Anthony and Carolyn are struggling with this issue. Their twenty-two-year-old son Benjie is blind and brain damaged, the result of a botched suicide attempt. "He was on drugs and had been drinking heavily when he shot himself in the head," Benjie's weary mother explains through her tears. "For seven years we tried to get him to change his lifestyle. We scolded, we punished, once we even called the police on him. Nothing worked. Now look at him. Just look at my son."

Forgive and forget? It isn't possible. We can and should work toward forgiveness, but we do not have the ability to erase memory from our minds.

Unconditional love? We can love mightily, but only God is capable of truly unconditional love.

The loss of the ability to lovingly empathize with the person in your care is a particularly cruel and torturous loss. Forgiveness is the Christian's way. It is not a choice; it is a commandment. We are to forgive as the Lord forgave us. (See Colossians 3:13; you will find that the benefits of forgiveness are more for you than for the person you are forgiving, by the way.) Start by asking God to make you willing to forgive and to give you a spirit of forgiveness. Ask him to impart to you an extra measure of love that you can pass on to the person in your care.

Where do you go from there? That depends both on you and on the other person. Is he repentant? Is he even capable of being repentant? Is there an option other than having the person under your sole care? Can the person live elsewhere—such as in a group home?

How about you? Can you bear to continue caring for the one who broke your heart? If you walk away, can you live with the consequences of that decision? How about if you stay? Can you truly live with that?

In a matter as soul-wrenching as this, you will need guidance from someone outside who can look at the situation with fresh, more objective eyes. Please, *please* talk with a counselor. Let that person help you decide how you will proceed.

When Jesus hung on the cross, crushed by the weight of our sins, he prayed, "Father, forgive them, for they do not know what they are doing" (Luke 23:34). Jesus understood every human weakness and selfish motivation of those who killed him. He knew that people act out of their own hurts and needs, which are often only dimly understood by others. He knew people choose not to see how their behavior affects others. He understood that they can inflict terrible pain when they wear blinders of denial, entitlement and wishful thinking.

You may think you understand the selfish motivations of the person you are caring for, but the truth is, none of us can ever really know another person's heart. In their book *Walk the Talk* Eric Harvey and Alexander Lucia write, "We judge others by their actions. We judge ourselves by our intentions." Whatever the actions of the person in your care, only God can look at his heart and see his intentions. Extend him this grace: pray along with our Lord, "Father, forgive him, for he didn't know what he was doing."

Grieve the Losses

"Lost hope? Absolutely not!" exclaims Patricia of her teenage son who broke his neck in a diving accident. "Jeff *will* get well! I refuse to admit to paralysis! I believe that God has let my son's prognosis look this bleak simply because he wants it to be a real miracle when he heals Jeff. It will be such a miracle that no one will be able to deny it was God and God alone who did it."

Sounds good. Very spiritual. Full of faith.

Not to Jeff, however. "Yes, I do believe God can heal me," he says in a resigned voice, "but I don't think he will." Then he adds, "My mother doesn't want to hear that, though. I don't think she wants a broken son."

For Patricia, clinging to hopes and chasing dreams—however unlikely—seems a triumphant way of life, especially when cloaked in words of faith. The fact is, Patricia is in denial. Pretending that everything is all right, she insists, means everything *will be* all right.

But where does that leave Jeff?

It is very important that we caregivers grieve our losses. Does that mean we have no faith? Absolutely not! Does it mean we aren't ready to accept healing from God? Not at all! But if we don't face reality, if we don't grieve our losses, the sorrows surrounding them will build up and build up until the burden becomes unbearable.

Grieving means acknowledging the pain of walking down a street and spotting a couple holding hands and laughing. It means allowing yourself to cry when you see a child just the age of your child, running and skipping. It means allowing those innocent, carefree acts to confront exactly what you have lost.

How About Spiritual Losses?

Accepting your losses does not mean you lose faith in God. Nor does it mean you must stop praying for healing. It simply means that you acknowledge the fact that you are neither greater nor wiser than God. You are praying for mercy and grace; you are also willing to accept his divine will.

You say that's awfully hard to do? It is. And yet that is the essence of faith in God.

Does your faith need strengthening? Here are some Scriptures that can help.

- Genesis 15:1-6: *God's promise to Abraham*
- Proverbs 3:5-9: *Wisdom God's way*
- Romans 5:1-11: *Our relationship to God through Christ*
- Hebrews 10:19-25: *He who promised is faithful*

Dealing with losses means

☐ honoring your memories of what used to be while you move on into what is

☐ living with resilience, not denial

☐ refusing to let denial stand in the way of finding creative options to meet the challenges of your life as a caregiver

☐ learning to balance your grief over what was lost with a recognition of what is still possible

☐ finding a way to express the loss you feel

☐ discovering a way to celebrate the gift your loved one is to you

☐ praying daily for wisdom and grace from above

The result of dealing with losses is worth it. Now you can go on to find the blessings!

11

Finding the Blessings

Larry and I had known Eileen and her husband, Phil, for years. We used to attend the same church. I didn't see them often anymore—mostly just when we ran into each other around town. Phil was a science professor at the university, and Eileen worked in a specialty shop downtown.

When I took Larry to the hospital for his first respite weekend, I was shocked to see Eileen there with Phil. Eileen looked the same as always, but I hardly recognized Phil. He was a wizened old man.

After checking our husbands in, Eileen and I went out for a cup of tea. We caught up on one another's kids, on our husbands' problems and prognoses, and we talked a bit about our lives as caregivers. Then we fell silent.

"It's so sad," I finally said. "Larry and Phil were so vital and so alive. Do you ever feel cheated?"

"No," Eileen said without hesitation. "I really don't. I've already experienced more love and joy in life than most people ever do. I think about that instead of what could have been."

Yes. That's it. Isn't that what the apostle Paul was saying? In Philippians

4:8 he wrote:

> Whatever is true, whatever is noble, whatever is right, whatever is pure, whatever is lovely, whatever is admirable—if anything is excellent or praiseworthy—think about such things.

Tears or Laughter

How good Eileen's perspective was! For quite a while I had been hearing one or another version of "For every minute of laughter, a caregiver has an hour of crying." The fact is, whatever the bad news, in its midst there is good news. It may be elusive, but it is there. Ask God to show it to you.

"Misfortune can still be worth a fortune." I heard that somewhere. I'm sure there is truth in that statement for anyone who is willing to dig deeply enough. But for Christians it is gospel truth. In his letter to the Romans the apostle Paul writes, "We know that God causes all things to work together for good to those who love him, to those who are called according to his purpose" (Romans 8:28).

Count It All Joy

Paul certainly knew his share of misfortunes. In fact, he was writing this very letter from prison! Paul suffered shipwreck, persecution, stoning, death threats, beatings—you name it. Church tradition tells us he was finally beheaded for his faith. And yet he writes this statement with such great confidence: it is God's intention to work *all* things together for good for those called to his purpose.

Knowing that God is at work weaving the events of my life together for good makes a huge difference in what I can endure. If I love God and have been called to his purpose, then I can be certain that he takes every single circumstance of my life and pieces it together to make something beautiful.

I take great comfort from the prayer David prayed after he was seized by the Philistines: "Thou hast taken account of my wanderings; Put my tears in Thy bottle; Are they not in the book? . . . This I know, that God is for me" (Psalm 56:8-9 KJV).

God works everything together for good. And he is for me. What peace these truths bring! And what joy!

"Well, I know what is happening to me," you may be saying, "and I can assure you it's not good!"

Not good by whose definition, yours or God's?

God's idea of good is diametrically opposed to what our society calls good. To see what God considers "good," look at Jesus' teachings in Matthew 5:1-12—what we know as the Beatitudes.

Good (blessed) are

- the poor in spirit
- those who mourn
- the meek
- those who hunger and thirst for righteousness
- those who are merciful
- the pure in heart
- the peacemakers
- those who are persecuted because of righteousness

To such people Jesus said, "Rejoice and be glad, because great is your reward in heaven."

My goal is to feel good, be happy, have in my life that which brings me pleasure and lets me avoid unpleasantness. God's goal is that I be conformed to the image of Christ.

The Source of Joy

To rest in God's sovereignty, to trust in his ability to cause *all things* that come into my life to work for good, is incredible. What freedom! What a source of joy! If all my difficult, painful experiences are being woven together for good, how can I despair? How can I question that the life of my afflicted loved one really does have meaning? I take great comfort in the words of Philip Yancey: "Faith means believing in advance what will only make sense in reverse."

"I don't get it," you may insist. "How can birth defects be good? Or accidents? Or disease? Or dementia?"

They aren't. Not in themselves. They are merely facts of the human condition. But God, in his infinite wisdom and love, takes all the events of our lives—both the good and the bad—and blending them together, ultimately works them for his intended good purpose.

Islands of Rest

Look for the islands of rest and hope in your life. They are there. Recall your happy memories. Relish them and take joy in them. Put together good times that family and friends can enjoy and remember. Laugh whenever you can, and don't feel guilty about it. Play recordings of songs of promise and encouragement. Write out encouraging verses and tape them up where you can see them often. Think on things that are true and noble and right and pure and admirable and excellent and praiseworthy. That's where you will find the places of relief.

Islands can spring up in unexpected places. Be ready to seize them whenever and wherever they appear—and in whatever form. Sometimes the experience is bittersweet, but not always. At times it is full, pure and rich. It can occur in a flash of insight when you see in your loved one's eyes a glimmer of true love and appreciation. It can come through a picture, a song, even an aroma that calls forth a memory that enlivens and refreshes you. It can come through laughter at an impossible situation.

When a joyful moment comes your way, don't take it for granted. Relish it and pack it away in your memory so that you can enjoy it again and again.

Islands of peace can come from offering peaceful moments to your loved one.

- Communicate with a soft touch.
- Speak with a gentle voice and soothing words.
- Sing songs to him or her.
- Hum as you work.
- Speak with whatever body language says peace in your family.

A Grateful Heart

Assume the position of a grateful heart. Make it a point to spend a few moments each day pondering the many things in your life for which you are thankful. Don't force yourself to give thanks for the pain in your life. With time that gratitude may come, but don't push it.

Again, let the psalmists lead you. Many psalms were written out of the depths of despair, and they are intended to be read by you during your depths of despair. Most of them don't supply answers to our problems. But when you read them, you will find that you are not alone. Someone else felt the way you feel and came through to sing about it.

Here are some psalms (KJV) to get you started:

I laid me down and slept; I awaked; for the LORD sustained me. (3:5)

Thou hast turned for me my mourning into dancing; thou hast put off my sackcloth, and girded me with gladness. (30:11)

Lord, all my desire is before thee; and my groaning is not hid from thee. (38:9)

For in thee, O LORD, do I hope: thou wilt hear, O Lord my God. (38:15)

I waited patiently for the LORD; and he inclined unto me, and heard my cry.
He brought me up also out of an horrible pit, out of the miry clay, and set my feet upon a rock and established my goings.
And he hath put a new song in my mouth, even praise unto our God. (40:1-3)

Don't allow the torrent of your tears to last too long. Rise up and read a psalm. Sing a song of praise. Do it even though you don't feel like it. You will be amazed at how quickly the Holy Spirit will bring you to a place of comfort and joy and peace.

Make it a regular practice to grasp your Father's outreached hand, and let him guide you to the islands of peace. Hold on tight, for there will be times when you can see nothing but rolling waves.

12

When Home
Is No Longer Possible

"I'M SORRY, MRS. STROM." THAT'S HOW THE DIRECTOR OF THE SHELTERED WORK-shop greeted me when I arrived for a hastily called conference. "We don't think your husband can continue here. His behavior has deteriorated markedly, and it is having a bad effect on our other workers. We have tried hard to accommodate him, but we just can't do it anymore."

I knew exactly what he meant. I too had seen that deterioration. Still, I was crushed. Larry's work time had already been cut to four hours three days a week. If he could no longer go at all, how was I going to manage?

Besides his increasingly disturbing behavior, he was more and more ob-stinate. Just the day before, a neighbor called to tell me that Larry was sit-ting in the middle of the street again. It took me fifteen minutes to coax him back into the house, and as soon as I turned my back he was trying to sneak out again. And he was getting more aggressive toward me. "Sorry," he would say with an impish grin after knocking me down, hitting me or dropping something on my foot.

A few nights later, a knife "slipped" out of his hand, flew across the room and lodged in the kitchen table beside me.

What was I going to do? Intending to plead for help, I made a list of the things that concerned and frightened me and took them to show Dr. Corazza after Larry's next appointment. But I never got around to showing him the list. I couldn't stop crying long enough. So I just sat across the desk in his office and sobbed. The only words I managed to get out were, "What am I going to do? *What am I going to do?*"

"That's it," Dr. Corazza said. "Larry needs to be out of the house."

There comes a time when loving family members have no choice but to turn the role of main caregiver over to professionals. It may happen when the afflicted person is no longer able to care for his most basic needs: bathing, eating, dressing, controlling his bladder and bowels. It may be because he has become a danger to himself, or it may be because he has become a danger to the people around him.

But what type of professional care is the best?

In-Home Care

One possibility is to get professional care in your home. This means that skilled nursing care and therapy will be provided at home on a regular, but not full-time, basis. Licensed nurses and therapists employed by public or private home care agencies come in and provide the care.

Home health services usually include such things as

☐ monitoring and assessing the patient's condition

☐ administrating medication, injections or other treatments, such as intravenous therapy or urinary catheterization

☐ taking care of wounds or injuries

☐ providing physical, occupational or speech therapy

☐ teaching patients and their caregivers how to perform specific tasks for themselves

In-home care has great advantages. It allows the person to remain at home. It lets the caregiver continue to provide whatever care he or she is able to. It puts off that major change to an entirely different type of living arrangement. For many caregivers who can no longer provide all the necessary care, it is a first option.

It also has disadvantages, however. First of all, it is often difficult to find adequate in-home help—most caretakers earn notoriously low wages. At the same time, it is expensive for the family, and most insurance policies don't cover it. (In some cases, however, Medicaid will help to cover the expenses, a route that is worth checking out.) It can also exact an emotional toll on caregivers, as it's awkward having someone else come into your house at any time.

Daycare

With the respite afforded by daycare away from home, many families are able to continue to handle their loved ones. There are nearly three thousand adult daycare programs throughout the country, and all indications are that they are becoming more available. Similar to children's daycare, adult daycare provides physical care, supervision and activities for adults who can't be left alone. Good programs offer stimulating activities, such as social events, exercise, art, music or perhaps even outings.

One disadvantage of daycare programs is that they tend to restrict their services to a specific type of person. Many take only seniors over the age of sixty-five. Others require that the person be ambulatory, or that she be continent (no diapers), or docile and nonaggressive. Some take only individuals who suffer from a particular disorder such as Alzheimer's disease or mental retardation.

But with the ever-expanding range of daycare options in many communities, it certainly is worth looking at what is available to you. (One of the best, most inclusive ones in our area is offered through a local church, an especially nice atmosphere.)

Group Homes

In some areas, group-care homes are available for certain adults. There may be anywhere from two to eight people in such a home. Generally a group home accepts those with one specific type of disability, such as developmentally challenged adults, Alzheimer's patients or elderly people with specific physical disabilities. In a good group home a person gets the advantages of companionship with other adults, and supervision and attention in a comfortable, homey atmosphere.

Since a person generally has to meet very specific guidelines to be accepted, it can be difficult to find an appropriate group home, but it is certainly worth looking and inquiring. Be sure to ask about cost since insurance, Medicare and Medicaid seldom cover group homes.

Nursing Homes

When we think of a person who is no longer able to live at home, the first picture that comes to mind is usually of a nursing home. And for most of us the thought is repugnant. The very term conjures up horrible pictures of warehoused old people tied to their wheelchairs, drugged and parked in smelly hallways to endure yet another day. Please try to set those pictures aside. Nursing homes have changed a lot in the past decade. Yes, there are still some bad ones. But there are also some very good ones where patients are offered personal care by an attentive staff and various stimulating activities to keep them busy and involved. Besides caring for the residents' physical needs, many offer a wide variety of recreational and social facilities including lounges, game rooms, crafts, libraries and beauty shops. The activities include church services, movies, bingo and other games, current events, various instructional and enrichment classes, music and entertainment. Also, many have social opportunities where family members can come and be involved with their loved ones in their loved ones' "homes." (Larry loved having guests join him in the monthly formal candlelight dinner.)

The care nursing homes provide is divided into two levels: *skilled care* and *intermediate care*. (Lesser levels of care are termed *residential*, but that refers more to a retirement type residence than to an actual nursing home.) These levels of care are defined in lengthy federal and state regulations, but basically this is what is involved:

☐ *Intermediate care* refers to a more basic level of care and is appropriate for patients who don't need intensive personal attention. It requires nurse supervision during the ordinary workweek dayshift, but at other times, care is provided by aides or practical nurses.

☐ *Skilled care* is a more intensive level of care. Here a registered nurse is available around the clock, seven days a week.

Most nursing homes provide both levels of care but in separate nursing units. This is an advantage because patients can go back and forth between the two as their condition changes.

How Can You Tell Good from Bad?

Nursing homes have felt a major sting of bad press. Without knowing anything firsthand many people start out prejudiced against them. (I was one of these people.) It's unfortunate because there are many fine physicians, nurses, social workers, aides, housekeepers, food service people, maintenance workers and other personnel who give their full devotion to the patients under their care. I know this from actual experience.

Each state conducts nursing-home inspections about once a year and issues a survey of its findings. This survey should be available at all nursing homes. Keep in mind that even a good home may be cited for deficiencies. The difference is that those deficiencies will likely be minor and will be fixed promptly.

Also, federal law requires each state to have an ombudsman's office where people can get impartial information. Ombudsmen visit nursing homes on a regular basis, and they have inside knowledge of what goes on in facilities in their communities. (The ombudsman I talked to told me about one nursing home just seven miles from my house. It was much less flashy than others in town, with attractive but simple landscaping. "It's the best kept secret in town," she told me.) Also, ombudsmen receive and investigate complaints made by or on behalf of nursing-home residents, and they work to resolve the problems. If they are unable to do so, or if they find serious violations, they refer the complaints to the state health department for action.

If you have trouble locating your local ombudsman, call the National Citizens' Coalition for Nursing Home Reform in Washington at (202) 332-2275.

Ask your ombudsman for

- information from the latest survey report on the facilities in your area
- any complaints against the nursing homes you plan to visit
- the number and nature of complaints for the past year
- the results and conclusions of the investigation into these complaints
- what to look for as telltale signs of good or poor care in the facilities

---

Armed with information from the ombudsman, you will want to personally visit each facility you are considering. It's a good idea to make these visits unannounced. (If a nursing home won't let you drop in, that should raise a red flag.) While you are there, keep your eyes open—also your ears and nose. Wander through the hallways, speak to residents and staff, as well as to any family members you may encounter. Look for clean, well-groomed residents. Listen for the staff's tone as they deal with the residents. See whether or not the nurses and aides mingle with them. Draw in a deep breath and consider the smells. Since many patients are incontinent, most nursing homes occasionally smell of urine, especially in the morning when the beds are being changed. But there should be no persistent stench or an overwhelming scent of cover-up air fresheners.

Talk to the administrator. You may need to make an appointment to come back and do this, but at least see if you can introduce yourself.

The nursing home should be a clean, busy, caring place even if the residents are not in prime shape. Be realistic. You cannot judge a nursing home's care by the same standards you might use for places that provide care for young, healthy individuals. I was shocked the first time I saw an elderly woman tied into her wheelchair with a sheet. But I soon learned that the alternative was to keep her confined to bed. When you see something that concerns you, don't be hesitant to ask: *When is it done? How is it done? Why is it done?* If the answer is logical, accept it. If it seems at all cold, superficial or unsatisfactory, challenge it.

There are some other things you'll need to find out about the particular facility.

☐ Is it close enough for family and friends to visit frequently?

☐ What services does it offer? Rehabilitation? Physical therapy? Social activities?

☐ What will it cost? In addition to the daily charges, find out about any added costs for wheelchairs, dental care, therapy, hand feeding, hair care, and so forth.

☐ What happens if your savings run out? Will your loved one be transferred somewhere else, or will the administrators help you apply for Medicaid?

☐ Are the nurses, aides and other employees well trained? Is there a physician on the staff either full-time or visiting on a regular basis?

☐ Are the buildings well maintained? Are the rooms comfortable and clean?

☐ What are the admission requirements for residents? Do you understand all the agreement's provisions?

If a facility passes your first inspection, plan to go back again at a different time. Bring along a copy of the checklist in appendix one and be prepared to make notes. It will help you compare one facility with another.

Making the Move
You have selected the care facility. Now how do you make the move as easy and comfortable as possible for your loved one?

First of all, don't expect the person to be happy about moving. She will almost certainly resist. She may plead, cry, threaten, even make hurtful remarks about you and your motives. You will undoubtedly feel terrible. You will question your own motives and feel guilty, selfish, even cruel. Yet if your decision was sound in the first place, it remains sound. So stand firm.

When I told Larry he was going to move, his parents were there to reinforce me. I tried to explain that with his difficulty swallowing and his increasing weakness, I just couldn't care for him by myself. His father agreed that the nursing home would be better for him. (I didn't mention his violent aggression. Larry would just say those incidents were accidents and dismiss it with "I told you I was sorry.")

Larry was very sad. He asked how long he would stay. I said I didn't know. He guessed, "Two years, two weeks and two days?" I answered, "Maybe so."

I moved Larry into room 332. I took his television along, put his clothes in the closet and drawers, hung a large frame with a collage of family pictures above his bed and took him a stuffed animal to sleep with. I put a telephone by his bed, programmed in my number and a few others, and told him he could call me whenever he wanted to. On his bulletin board I hung the menu, and I read it to him. I also posted a list of activities and chattered cheerfully as I circled the most interesting ones.

Larry said he didn't care about any of that. And I could tell it was true—he didn't. Leaving him there, sunken into a corner of his bed looking lost and forlorn with his stuffed bear clutched close, was the hardest thing I've ever done. "I'll be back tonight," I promised. "And I'll come back every day. And I'll call, too." Then I left.

That night I moped through dinner. "I think I made a terrible mistake today," I said miserably to Patrick, the young college student who was staying with us. Then I told him all about the afternoon.

"Well," Patrick said, "when we finish eating, let's go see how he's doing."

When we got to Larry's room, he was happily propped up in bed watching television and eating ice cream. "This is great!" he told us. "I can eat all I want, and I don't have to do anything I don't want to do! This is a good place to live."

"This is how it usually goes," one of the nurses told me on our way out. "The first day, maybe even the first week, is hard. But then they settle in. They make friends with the staff and with other residents, and they see the advantages of being here."

Your loved one's transition may not be as quick as Larry's was. Just continue to reassure her that you are not deserting her. Plan ahead for several visits or outings. Look through the week's scheduled activities and help her to anticipate what the next day has in store for her.

Once your loved one is settled in, you will both feel much better about it. There will be those people who will say such a thing as "I guess it's okay for you, but I could never put someone I love in a place like that." Well, they have no way of knowing what they would do if they were in your situation, and don't hesitate to tell them so.

Even with your loved one in a nursing home, you are still the caregiver. Although your responsibilities have changed, you are no less crucial a part of her life.

☐ *Visit often and regularly.* One of the saddest things at the nursing home was seeing disabled and elderly people get all dressed up and wait expectantly in the front lobby for visitors who never showed up. If you are unable to make your visit, call the nursing station and ask that your loved one be notified.

Drop in at various times of the day. Human nature being what it is, residents with attentive families who visit regularly tend to receive better treatment than those who have no one to check up on their care.

You can do several things to help your loved one acclimate more quickly:

- *Make her room hers.* Her room—or her side of the room—should have a personal touch. Ask if you can bring her pillow or her reading lamp. (Larry especially wanted his bed backrest and his stuffed bear.) Have some family pictures to display. Bring books and magazines she likes. Bring her Bible. Having her own things around will help her feel safe and more in control.

- *Visit frequently, but* ... Experts tell us you shouldn't visit constantly right away. I know. You'll worry if you aren't there. You'll feel guilty. But if you are always there to do everything and make all the decisions, she won't need to handle this change herself. As best you can, put away your guilt and anxiety. When you do visit, come ready with things to talk about and be open to listen to her. Go for a walk together. At first it will be hard for both of you, but do the best you can.

- *Get an autograph book.* "No one ever comes to see me!" your loved one may insist. It will help to get her a guest book and put it out on her bedside table. Encourage people to sign in and leave a message. Children can scrawl their names or draw pictures. Now and then you can show her the book and read the messages to her. Larry took great pleasure in showing his book to everyone who came by, whether he knew them or not.

- *Bring treats.* Larry loved the food at the nursing home, but he lived for his treats: peanut butter and jelly, raisins, cheddar cheese puffs, his favorite cold cereals. I brought them, and also fresh fruit, enough for both of us, and we ate it together. If your loved one complains about the food, why not have a meal with her now and then? If possible, occasionally take her out to eat, or bring her favorite foods in to her.

- *Get to know the staff.* Be friendly and say hello. Spend time talking to them, especially the head of nursing. The better you know the people who care for your loved one every day, the more you'll hear about what's happening in her life. I tried to do something special for the staff every other month or so (homemade cookies, greeting cards, flower bouquets). Let them know the things about them you appreciate. They certainly hear all the negatives, so something positive is always appreciated—and remembered.

☐ *Play together.* Discover what your loved one does for fun and join in. Listen to her music. Watch a movie at the nursing home together. Go play bingo with her. Attend her classes. And whenever possible, be there for special times. In the summer, Larry's home had lunchtime barbecues on Fridays. Larry loved for me to come and eat hamburgers with him and his friends.

☐ *Phone her from home.* If you don't live near enough to your loved one to visit, telephone regularly. Even if she doesn't like to talk on the phone. Even if she doesn't speak well. Even if she has nothing to say. Periodically talk with the head of nursing about your loved one and her progress. Also write to her often. Send along pictures, drawings, comics, interesting newspaper clippings.

☐ *Visit by proxy.* If you live far away, find a friend or relative who lives near the nursing home who will go by now and then.

☐ *Know the doctor.* Know how to reach your loved one's doctor, even if you are far away. It will be comforting to her to know you can get in touch with the physician if you need to.

☐ *Bring photographs.* Pictures and photo albums are fun to look through together. On one visit a friend brought along an album of pictures of her trip to Russia. Larry loved it!

☐ *Bring music.* If you play a musical instrument, bring it. Larry's roommate's granddaughter brought her flute one day. We all enjoyed her playing, and her grandpa beamed with pride.

☐ *Go outside.* Take your loved one out of doors. The fresh air will be a nice change, and it will be good for her to see the world outside. Point out the birds and listen to them sing. Encourage her to smell the flowers. Admire God's handiwork together.

☐ *Treat her to a manicure or pedicure.* Not only will this keep the person well groomed, it will also be soothing and comforting to her. Bring clippers, an emery board and some rich lotion.

☐ *Give a massage.* A neck, back or whole body massage with fragrant lotion is so relaxing, and nothing is as comforting as the human touch. Regular massages also gave me an opportunity to check over Larry's body. Since he didn't feel pain, and he carefully hid any injuries, small wounds would become infected before anyone knew he had even hurt himself. Several times I found abscesses on his feet and legs.

☐ *Spend time on his terms.* I wanted to converse with Larry, and to share thoughts and concerns with him. But it soon became clear that wasn't going to work. After a few minutes of strained talk, he would say, "*Now will you read to me?*" So that's what we did, day after day, month after month, year after year. It may not be what you would choose, but spend time with your loved one on his terms.

☐ *Be ready with suggestions for others.* Many times people don't visit because they don't know what to do or say. If you can give them ideas, it will help them be more at ease visiting. (I would suggest people bring a short article or devotion to read to Larry, or a word search or easy crossword puzzle to help him do.)

☐ *Make yourself part of her world.* Your loved one's world has changed. You will be more relevant to her if you become a part of her world. One Thanksgiving my friend Gerda and I reserved a room at the nursing home and set up a lovely table. I invited several of Larry's friends at the home and an on-duty nurse to join us for Thanksgiving dinner. We gave thanks together, each shared a special Thanksgiving memory, and we had a nice meal. Afterward Larry said, "I'm glad we did this at my house this year."

Yes, you do have to relate differently now. But in some ways, it can be better. Instead of having to scold, fix and coerce, you can relax and enjoy your time together. You can search out the vital person inside that helpless-looking body and treat your loved one with the dignity he deserves.

But I Feel So Guilty

When Larry hit that curb and fell off his bike, breaking his teeth and nose, and requiring eleven stitches to close the gash on his chin, I felt many things during the hours I spent in the emergency room and the dentist's office, but one thing I did not feel was guilty for having him there. Why would I? He was in the hands of capable professionals who knew how to help him. And yet I did feel guilty when he went into the nursing home. It made no sense. The nursing home was also staffed by capable professionals. They too were able to give him the care he needed.

Our guilt feelings have nothing to do with making sense. They are more emotional than rational. We feel we are deserting our loved ones by not continuing on as their sole caregivers.

Make a decision that you will not submit to that unfair emotion. There is no reason for you to feel guilty. You are, after all, still caring for your loved one. Just because you have placed him in the hands of professionally trained nursing home personnel doesn't mean you are no longer a caring participant in his life.

I was amazed at the peace that came to Larry after he moved into the nursing home. No longer did he have to struggle to try to "fit in" and "act right." He formed a circle of friends with whom he was comfortable, and before long his friends became my friends. I brought chocolate for Mary, sang with Kathleen, joked with Gary, brought crossword puzzles for Earlene and shopped for Lyle. And every Sunday afternoon I attended their church and worshiped with them.

Let me tell you about that church.

Everyone came in whatever way they felt comfortable. It was not a fashion show there. Volunteers Les and Dorothy played the piano and organ, and Donald led the singing. We sang all the old gospel hymns, and when we finished singing a favorite like "Amazing Grace," someone would start over, and we would sing the whole song through again. Once we sang "The Old Rugged Cross" four times. No one complained.

An old, bent lady named Mimi always sang a solo. It wasn't particularly tuneful, but no one cared about that either. Anybody who knew the words chimed in and sang along with her.

Donald read Scripture and gave a short sermon. We always knew when Earlene agreed with him because she did so in a loud, enthusiastic voice.

Larry and I sat on the couch (most people were in wheelchairs), and when it was time to sing, I helped everyone find the right page in their hymn booklets. Larry proudly told everyone I was the "church room mother." I guess I was.

Once Larry was in the nursing home and the entire responsibility for his care was off me, I was able to relax and enjoy my time with him more than I had for years. "I like my home," Larry once told me. "I think they built this place just for me."

Perhaps they did.

13

There Is Only
So Much Money

LARRY HAD ALWAYS BEEN THE MAIN WAGE EARNER IN OUR FAMILY. I HAD WORKED part-time as a substitute teacher, but the money I earned went to pay for vacations, special projects around the house, and—we had planned—for college expenses for the children. When Larry could no longer work, the entire financial burden fell on me—and that was the year our second child started college. We had a house to rebuild, all our belongings to replace, two children in college and no income from Larry. I couldn't teach because I couldn't leave Larry alone. I had been writing, but all my work was lost in the fire, including two books I had already been paid for that now had to be rewritten.

We needed money!

Long-term illness is enormously expensive. The very rich have the resources to pay their own bills. The very poor have the government. But those in between—and that's the majority of us—discover that a long illness can wipe us out.

I soon learned that every caregiver gets a new hobby—filling out medical claim forms!

From the beginning I struggled with the processors for our medical insurance. I reasoned, cajoled, pleaded and downright begged them for help. In desperation I turned to threats (the state insurance commissioner first, then I had a lawyer friend write a well-worded letter on his letterhead). I started out sweet and nice and reasonable, but I toughened up real quick.

On top of all the other anguish, the caregiver gets the added burden of dealing with the terrifying possibility of financial impoverishment. Most medical insurance doesn't cover home custodial care for those with incurable illnesses. There may not be reimbursement for psychologists or therapists. Medicare will sometimes pay for a nurse to come in to give an injection or dress a wound, but the backbreaking, night-and-day routine of feeding, dressing, changing sheets and dealing with the person's behavior is up to the family.

For us, nursing-home care was a real killer financially. Nursing-home costs now average around $100 a day, which adds up to a whopping $36,500 a year, and it continues to go up every year. And no, most insurance doesn't pay it. Nor, with very few exceptions, does Medicare.

Sheltering Your Assets

As the law now stands, you must pay out of your own pocket until you're impoverished enough to qualify for Medicaid. How poor you have to be depends on where you live. The limits are adjusted for inflation, and they vary from state to state. (For us, Larry could keep no more than $2,000 in assets. I, as the healthy spouse of such a person, was allowed to keep approximately $75,000. Not much of a nest egg for the rest of my life!)

Some assets, however, aren't counted in those totals, so the best thing you can do is to move as much money as possible into exempt categories.

Is this legal? Absolutely. As in any such program, there are those people who juggle the laws and take unfair advantage of what is allowed. Tips on how to shelter your assets and still qualify for Medicaid are the stuff of hot-selling self-help books, financial-planning seminars and even adult education courses. But the intent of the law is to allow care for a family member without totally bankrupting the family. The point is to *use* the protection offered you, not to *abuse* it.

Laws vary from state to state, and they change frequently. Also, the details of one person's situation is different from those of another. It is important that you get a professional to help you navigate your way through the choppy legal waters. A nursing-home social worker can give you some guidance; even better is a lawyer who specializes in elder care. The following information, however, will help you get an idea of where you are going and will enable you to start putting together a list of questions. Here are some protections you should know about.

Your house. One of the best shelters is a home. In most states a family's primary residence is exempt so long as the spouse or dependent children live there. There is no limit on the value of that home. A multimillion dollar mansion is just as exempt as a small mobile home.

So consider

☐ paying off your mortgage if you possibly can

☐ replacing your home with a bigger one

☐ investing in home improvements: repaint, recarpet, build an addition, landscape the yard

Household goods. Many states don't count the value of household goods either. (Although some draw the line at such "extravagances" as antique furniture and expensive art.)

So consider

☐ buying a new refrigerator or other appliances you need

☐ replacing old furniture with new

One car. A spouse is also allowed to keep one car. Again, it makes no difference how expensive it is.

So consider

☐ trading in your old clunker for a reliable car

☐ investing in a car that retains its value

Irrevocable trusts. An irrevocable trust is sheltered, but before you put your assets into one, you need to consult with an attorney. While a nursing home can't touch the principal on such a trust, neither can you.

So consider

☐ an irrevocable trust (*but* get good legal advice before pursuing it)

Some Things Are Not Sheltered

Here are some things you should know are *not* sheltered.

A nursing-home resident's own income. If the person you are caring for gets a pension, social security check, dividends from stocks or bonds, or money from any other source, it will go toward paying the nursing-home bill. You can, however, keep any income that comes in your own name.

A second car. Actually, any second vehicle (motor home, pick up truck) is not sheltered.

A second home. If you have a second home, a vacation cabin in the woods or a rental house, it is not exempt.

Think carefully and prayerfully about what you can and should shelter. I didn't want to take unfair advantage of the system, and at the same time I was haunted by the question: If I end up wiped out, how will I provide for my children and support myself for the rest of my life?

Make Use of What's Available

So where can you look for financial aid? Here are some places to consider.

Private insurance. Enlist the help of the benefits specialist at work (if it's a group policy) or even an attorney to make sure you are getting all that your insurance policy allows. You cannot depend upon the insurance company to bring anything to your attention. For instance, Larry's life insurance policy had a rider that stipulated that should he become totally disabled, we wouldn't have to pay any more premiums. I would never have claimed it if his father hadn't brought it to my attention. Once you know what you are entitled to, don't take no for an answer. Insurance companies are great at wearing you down with arguments and delays. Stand firm and insist. As a last resort you may decide to threaten legal action.

There are Medicare supplementary insurance policies that promise to bridge the gap between "real costs" and what Medicare covers. There is also private, long-term care insurance available. These options don't help much when the person is already disabled, however.

Social Security. Many chronically ill patients may qualify for Social Security disability benefits. If a person applies and is denied, he or she may apply for reconsideration. If the reconsideration is also denied, the person may appeal to the office of hearings and appeals. "If a person has a definable disease that will disable him for twelve months or more, then his chances of qualifying for social security benefits are good," we were told.

Unfortunately, Larry's illness was not "definable." Chorea acanthocytosis is too rare and unknown to be listed in their book. He was denied the benefits, and I appealed. The woman who came out to our house and interviewed us told me later, "We really challenge a claim when the person is under fifty and has a college education. We feel they can usually do *something* to earn money." But she agreed Larry could not and helped me get the Social Security he was due.

It can take as long as a year to go from the initial application to the court hearing. "A lot of people don't know they can appeal," the woman who helped us told me. "Only a small percentage who are denied go on to have a hearing. If more people knew they could appeal, a lot more would get their benefits."

Medicare. A federal insurance program for people sixty-five and older, Medicare also covers the disabled. It is composed of two parts, Part A and Part B. Part A is hospital insurance, and Part B is medical insurance. You can get information about Medicare through your local Social Security office. Since it is strictly a federal program, the rules are the same throughout the United States.

In certain instances Medicare may cover a part of home health care for patients who are confined to their homes and some skilled nursing care, or physical or speech therapy. These services are limited and must be ordered and regularly reviewed by a medical doctor, and must be provided by a Medicare-certified home health agency. Participating home health agencies can assess the case of the person in your care at no charge and let you know whether or not she is eligible for Medicare-covered home health services. These services may include

☐ home health-aide services to assist with personal care (eating, bathing, dressing)

☐ medical social services, such as counseling, under the direction of a doctor

☐ medical supplies and equipment (covering up to 80 percent of the cost of durable medical equipment, such as wheelchairs)

Medicare does *not* cover full-time care, housekeeping services or food services. Nor does it cover more than a very limited stay in a nursing home, and then only if the patient is transferred directly from a hospital stay. Unfortunately the majority of Medicare users mistakenly believe that it does cover long-term care and that they are automatically protected. Then when a protracted illness strikes, they—or their families—are devastated.

Medicaid. This cooperative federal-state assistance program provides health care services to low income and "needy" people. Since the program is run by the state health or welfare agency under the general guidelines of the federal government, income guidelines and rules vary from state to state.

Medicaid does pay for nursing-home care in certified homes and for qualified patients. Because the cost of nursing-home care is so high, sooner or later most people without appropriate insurance end up here, many times after the costs have gutted any life savings they may have had. (Hence the idea of "spending down" to qualify.) Nursing homes aren't supposed to "dump" Medicaid patients out to make room for private payers (many of whom pay almost double what Medicaid pays), or to refuse to accept them in the first place. But in most states, competition for Medicaid beds is brisk and waiting lists can be long.

Nursing-home personnel, the Department of Welfare, the Department of Health or the Department of Human Resources should all be able to help you find information about, and show you how to apply for, Medicaid.

There may be other programs through which you qualify for financial aid. Consider:

- *SSI (Supplemental Security Income).* This is administered through the Social Security Administration. You can find out more about it by calling the Social Security Office in your area.

- *Veterans Administration.* Some veterans are eligible for short-term and long-term care. Call the Veterans Administration in your area for further information.

- *Workers Compensation.* This program covers the major needs that arise from a work-related accident or illness. You can get information on this program through the person's employer or through your state's department of labor.

Help!

During my search for financial relief, my counselor at the Social Services Department told me, "If you were smart, you would stop working and just go on welfare. It would be a lot easier, and you would come out ahead financially."

Stop working? Stop trying? How could I look in the faces of my friends—and even of strangers, for that matter—knowing they were working to pay taxes to support me and pay my husband's expenses when I was still perfectly capable of working?

As a Christian and a responsible citizen I firmly believe we have every right to use the services to which we are entitled. I also feel strongly that we have no right to take advantage of our situations. God has called us to be responsible stewards of what he has entrusted us with.

Certainly caregiving is a full-time job. And it may be that your own health, either physical or emotional, is an issue that prevents you from working. By all means look into what is available from the government that can benefit you. Even if you do continue to work, the government may still offer you some assistance. (They paid a portion of Larry's nursing-home costs.)

Being a faithful steward can mean giving and it can mean receiving. In both ways, determine to be a faithful steward.

14

Letting Go

I'M NOT SURE WHETHER IT'S MY PERSONALITY, MY UPBRINGING OR A COMBINA-tion of things, but I have always been a person who sees a goal and dog-gedly works toward it. I have trouble being patient with people who sit by, shrug their shoulders and say, "It's out of my hands. Why try?"

Larry, on the other hand, was always a much more laid-back, let's-just-see-how-it-goes type of person.

Early on in his disease, the therapists gave us a list of things Larry could do to keep his body and mind working to the maximum for as long as pos-sible. Besides physical exercises, it included working puzzles, doing math problems, reading and doing practical things like cooking (following a rec-ipe) and being responsible for household tasks.

To me the course of action seemed obvious: do those things. And do them again. If it's good to do them once a day, why not twice? Or three times?

But Larry saw if differently. "It's not fun," he told me. "I don't want to do those things if they aren't fun."

I pushed; Larry balked. I prodded; Larry dug in his heels. I nagged;

Larry closed his eyes and went to sleep.

"I've got to push him!" I cried out in exasperation. "I've got to make him try!"

I look back on those difficult, tumultuous times, and I wonder: If Larry had really tried, I mean *really tried*, would it have made a difference? In the short run perhaps it may have. But in the long run probably not. Either way, the fact was, *Larry didn't want to do it*. It may well be that he wasn't even capable of wanting to. At any rate, I couldn't make him do anything. Nor (even harder for me to accept) could I make him *want* to.

A Time to Push, A Time to Stop

There is a time to push, and there is a time to stop pushing. There is a time to challenge and a time to accept. There is a time to cling tight and a time to loosen your grip. There is a time to hold on and a time to let go.

Sometimes we can do nothing but let go.

Then comes the time to grieve.

The Cycle of Grief

Ever since Swiss-born psychiatrist Dr. Elisabeth Kubler-Ross coined the DABDA cycle of grief (denial, anger, bargaining, depression, acceptance), it has been a model that, to one degree or another, has been accepted by many counselors and psychologists around the world. Certainly grief does not come in a neat little package. It's not a question of "go through the cycle and get it over." Nor will you necessarily go through the stages in order. You may even go back and forth between them. It can take years to make it through your grief, and it must be done at your own pace and in your own way.

"I have no one to grow old with," Eileen lamented. "No one to aggravate me, to kiss me goodnight, to move the furniture I can't lift." After a pause she added, "I have no one anymore. How can I ever get over a grief like this?"

Maybe she can't. Her grief may never fully disappear. But by working through her grief, Eileen, just like you and like me, can move forward toward a happy, useful future.

Let's look at the DABDA cycle.

Denial

In the denial stage we refuse to believe what's happening. Symptoms go by unnoticed or unacknowledged. When we are informed that something is very wrong, we insist, "There must be some mistake."

Larry and I stayed in this stage too long. Without others to confirm a problem, it was easy to simply deny it existed. (Larry said, "Nothing's wrong." I said, "Stop acting like this, Larry!")

A stage of denial is natural and good. It is a defense mechanism that helps us handle the shock. But to stay in this stage too long can prevent us from getting the medical or emotional help we need.

Anger

After denial comes anger. Anger can be turned inward toward ourselves, or it can be turned outward, where it strikes out at others.

Turned inward anger takes the form of false and/or legitimate guilt. We may cry out, "It's all my fault! If only I had . . ."

Turned outward, anger takes on the appearance of an incensed reaction toward someone else: "It's *your* fault this happened! You were driving the car!" There can be many different targets for anger turned outward. One target can be God himself: "He couldn't be a God of love! If he was, how could he let this happen?"

The problem with this stage of grief is that anger can quickly grow into bitterness, and bitterness into hatred. Whether directed at ourselves, at another or at God, anger is a powerful time bomb. It needs to be carefully defused before someone gets terribly hurt.

Bargaining

People who have never in their lives acknowledged God turn to him in their grief and attempt to strike a bargain: "God, if you will only heal him, I promise I will . . ." We remind God of all we have done for him. We argue, reason, propose deals, plead. And to prove our point we become "supergood" and unusually cooperative with everyone around us.

Depression

This fourth stage of grief is a time of tears and unspeakable sadness. There are days when we can barely pull ourselves out of bed. We don't care whether or not we eat or how we look. It just doesn't matter anymore. Life hardly seems worth living.

The person who is ill may experience this depression in a way totally unexpected. Some act out in anger, others completely withdraw. (Larry took to sleeping all night and a good part of the next day.)

Although we can expect a certain amount of depression, coming to a place of complete or sustained withdrawal, or to where we can no longer function, is a signal that we or our loved ones need help.

Acceptance

Once we have worked through the previous stages, acceptance comes almost automatically. For us as Christians, it is here that the promises of God's word produce a renewed confidence and trust in God's wisdom and love. "This has happened," you can say. "I don't like it, but I can deal with it. And I will be stronger because of God's faithfulness in bringing me through it." With acceptance we finally have peace of mind, and our joy and pleasure in life begins to return.

How can we come to the place where we can open our hands and our hearts so that we can begin to let go? Here are some suggestions of ways to begin:

- In a notebook or journal, write as if you are speaking to your loved one. Put down all those things you can't express in person. Write about anything and everything—the things you did together, the places you visited, even his habits that annoyed you.

- If you have children, write a journal for them. Write it as if the afflicted person is speaking to them. Let "him" express the things he would want your children to remember about him.

- Find one close friend with whom you can spend quality time on a regular basis, then do it.

- Cherish your friends who treat you with patience, understanding, love and care. Hold close those who care enough to really listen and who love you enough to tell you what you need to hear.

- Don't neglect worship and fellowship. They are like food and water to you. They will bless and nourish your soul.

There was a time shortly before Larry went into the nursing home when I believed there was an even chance I would die at his hands. He didn't act angry, but in a frighteningly detached way he hit me and knocked me down "accidentally." It continued even after he went into the nursing home; in time I was under doctor's orders not to be alone with him. Yet at the same time he seemed too vulnerable and sad to be alone. I got my affairs in order and wrote final letters to my children. "Your will be done," I told God. I was too tired to argue. If I died, I thought with my befuddled reasoning, I would ask Jesus for a soft heavenly bed where I could sleep for a few dozen years.

God's will was done. He got through to me, and I finally gave up my grip on the situation I couldn't really control at all. I let go.

"Letting God" has a lot to do with letting go.

Letting go is taking the advice of Jesus, who tells us again and again to look beyond this temporary world to the eternal world beyond. It forces us to rethink our priorities and to reconsider our Christian life. Whatever happens here in this life, we have the assurance that we are in the hands of a loving Shepherd who will gently guide us along the black and winding trail through the valley of the shadow of death.

You will have days when you feel you are doing well. You will have days when you feel the bottom has fallen out of your life. But like the winter that always breaks into spring, so will the winter of your life one day blossom again.

When you are called upon to struggle with grief and loss, allow God's grace and comfort to carry you through. "I learned that your family members are only on loan to you," Toni said. "They are God's. And he loves them more than you do."

Fear thou not; for I *am* with thee: be not dismayed; for I *am* thy God: I will strengthen thee; yea, I will help thee; yea, I will uphold thee with the right hand of my righteousness. (Isaiah 41:10 KJV)

15

A Time for
Every Purpose

"Do you have legal power of attorney so that you can make health care decisions for Larry?" Dr. Corazza asked me.

Did I? I wasn't sure.

"Do it now while he is still cooperative," he insisted. "The time will come when he won't be."

I didn't want to consider such things as power of attorney, wills and changing bank accounts into my name. I didn't want to talk about it, I didn't want to think about it, and I certainly didn't want to do it.

But it was time.

A Time to Find an Attorney

Now, at whatever point you are, start preparing by locating a good attorney.

Ask friends, business associates, even your pastor, for referrals. Certainly you can find plenty of lawyers listed in your local telephone book, but you will likely feel more confident with a referral from a trusted source.

To find a Christian attorney in your area, you can contact

Christian Legal Society
P.O. Box 1492
Merrifield, Virginia 22116
(703) 642-1070

Once you get a few names, call and inquire as to the attorney's specialty, experience, expertise and fees. (It would be especially good to find one with experience in elder care.) Just talk to a secretary on this initial contact. Lawyers are notorious for charging per minute.

Once you decide on an attorney, call and make an appointment. Then get to work and do your homework. Get together everything you need to go over with the attorney. Write out your questions and concerns. The better you prepare, the less time it will take in the office, and the less it will cost you. Here are some things you might want to talk over with the attorney.

Preparing a Will

Larry and I had wills drawn up when our first child was born. But it suddenly occurred to me that should I die first, everything would go to him, and he was in no condition to handle it. Also, if he was in a nursing home, everything would go for his care there, leaving nothing for the children's education or to continue to meet his uncovered needs. I was the one who really needed the new will.

Actually, it makes sense for anyone to have an up-to-date will properly prepared. It can save lengthy legal tie-ups in probate and can also prevent legal battles among family members. Basically what a will does is make sure a person's desires, rather than the state's, are accomplished in regard to his or her estate and personal affairs.

Assigning Power of Attorney

The power of attorney simply means one person gives another the power to conduct business on his or her behalf. This power can be limited to a one-time project, such as selling a house or handling a bank account, or it can be a general power of attorney that would give unlimited control over all aspects of that person's affairs. The terms of the document determine how much power is given over. It can be written to encompass whatever issues one chooses. It can take effect as soon as the ink is dry, or it can spring into action when specific circumstances arise. (As Larry's condition deteriorated, both the hospital and the nursing home required that I show proof of a signed durable power of attorney for his health care. Fortunately I had followed the doctor's advice and gotten it done. By the time I needed it, Larry was so suspicious and paranoid that he never would have agreed to it.)

There are two categories of durable powers of attorney: one for financial matters and another for health care issues. The financial durable power of attorney gives the person acting on your behalf access to checking, savings and investment accounts. The health care durable power of attorney allows him or her to provide for your care and well being, or to have medical care—including life support—terminated according to your written wishes.

Standard power of attorney forms can be purchased at a stationery store. For your own protection, however, and for that of your loved one, it might be wise to have an attorney draw up the document. That way, proper wording and clauses dealing with your specific circumstances can be included. If you decide to do it yourself, be sure to have your signatures notarized so that there is no question as to their validity.

Guardianship

You cannot legally be given power of attorney by a person who doesn't have the mental capacity to understand what he is doing. Should your loved one become too impaired, someone—perhaps you—may be appointed guardian or conservator. This involves the painful process of having the courts declare your loved one incompetent.

I can tell you from personal experience that this is one of the most painful things you will ever have to do. In Larry's case he could not legally be "locked in" the nursing home against his will, and he was determined to leave, get a car and drive to Sweden. He wasn't rational, but the nursing home could no longer be responsible for him. And short of having a guardianship declared, there was nothing I could do either.

If a guardianship is needed, get it. And don't second guess your decision (*"Did I do the right thing?"*) or accept criticism from others (*"I could never do something like that to someone I love!"*). Punishing yourself accomplishes nothing.

Protect Your Loved One

Rita, thirty-two, has Down syndrome. All her life she has lived with her parents. "What will happen to her after we die?" her mother, Barbara, worries. "Or what if we become incapacitated? Who will care for her?"

Because of improved medical care, there is a growing population of people with developmental disabilities, including those who are afflicted by mental retardation, autism and cerebral palsy. Planning for their lifelong care has become a challenge for many parents.

AARP (American Association of Retired Persons) has a list of resources and organizations dedicated to helping the caregivers of such individuals. Write and request *Facts about Adult Children with Developmental Disabilities and Their Families*. (See appendix two for the address.) You may also want to check out AARP's website at <http://www.aarp.org>.

A Time for Informed Financial Planning

If you think only rich people need or can afford financial advisers, think again. Everyone needs good financial advice. A capable tax accountant, financial planner, lawyer, stockbroker or insurance agent can save you thousands of dollars by helping you avoid common, costly mistakes. Now that you are responsible for someone who is depending on you for care—not to mention your other financial responsibilities (saving for college, buying or selling a house, choosing an insurance policy, stressing over your tax return, planning your retirement)—you will need all the help you can get.

Good advice doesn't have to be back-breakingly expensive. The hourly fees of financial planners, for example, range from $75 to $250, and a couple of hours of advice may be all you need. A financial planner's main job isn't to manage your money. It's to help you figure out where you stand financially, to analyze your needs and goals, and to help you create a plan to meet them.

A Time to Die

Many of us are dealing with caregiving situations that will end in the death of our loved ones. While some may want to discuss plans for their funeral, others will refuse to talk about it. Although Larry wouldn't discuss it, I talked with him about what I wanted for myself and was able to make some decisions for him based on how he responded.

One of the worst ways to handle this is to wait until your loved one dies and then find yourself at the mercy of funeral home personnel. Make the arrangements when you are able to think clearly and not feel pressured.

Long ago Larry and I agreed that we wanted to be cremated and have our ashes scattered at sea. Yet when I went to the funeral home to make advance arrangements, I was hit with a nonstop sales pitch. ("Doesn't your husband deserve the very best? Let me show you our deluxe casket model, all mahogany and brass. Just imagine him resting in peace and comfort on these satin pillows.") A modest funeral costs about $3,000 in the United States, but it's possible to spend one tenth—or ten times—that amount. You can easily get pulled into spending a great deal more than you intend or can afford. The more stressed you are, the more your guilt and emotions will overrule your good sense.

Death Benefits

It's good to know ahead of time what benefits you will have to help with the costs when the time comes. The most common benefit will be your loved one's life insurance policy. Social Security is also a possibility. If your loved one is a veteran, that may be another option. Veteran death benefits for honorably discharged veterans may include burial space in a government-owned cemetery, a burial allowance, a headstone or marker, a burial flag and possibly even a pension for the survivors.

Preplan the Service

Preplanning minimizes the stress when the death occurs. You will be able to choose exactly the kind of service you want. I had sat down with the pastor and discussed everything including what songs were to be sung (Larry's favorite hymn, "Like a River Glorious," and a solo sung in Swedish by a dear friend), the Scripture that was to be read (his favorite passage, 1 Corinthians 13), who would speak (our son and Larry's father) and an idea of what the minister was to say.

The funeral director can be another source for helping you make decisions about the service.

If Death Occurs at Home

One of my greatest fears was that Larry would die at home. I had no idea what I would do. If this is a possibility, it would be a good idea to talk this over with the doctor and the funeral director. I was told that the best response would be to call 911. Paramedics would respond quickly and take over, either taking the person to the hospital or contacting the coroner. The coroner would ask which mortuary was preferred.

If Death Occurs in a Hospital

The attending physician will take over and will sign the death certificate. A hospital social worker will meet with you to determine if there are some immediate family members who should be contacted and will ask if there is anything else he or she can do to help. The social worker will advise you how to proceed with contacting the mortuary.

Whether death comes suddenly, or occurs at an unexpected time in the course of a disability, or comes as a blessed relief at the end of a long illness, it will be hard. It is difficult to think rationally or to make good decisions in even the most mundane of matters.

After the death of your loved one

- Make sure the appropriate people are notified. Ask someone close to you to help you with that. (Gerda helped me, and so did my pastor.)

- Set aside one drawer (or box) in which to put any letters or papers that may be important. In the confusion that follows a death, they have a way of getting misplaced. Later you can go through the drawer and sort everything out.

- Dispose of the person's medications. (In many cases it's safer to flush them than to just throw them away. Call your pharmacy and ask about the best way to dispose of them.)

- Get a notebook and write down every call you make or receive: who called, the date, the phone number, the purpose of the call. In anything official, get the name of the person to whom you speak.

- Keep a list of all the gifts, remembrances, flowers, gifts to charities, or anything special you want to remember and acknowledge. A personal note to each giver means so much, however, it is perfectly all right to use the little preprinted thank you cards the mortuary provides.

- Accept offers to help. If people don't offer, ask. Most people really do want to help, but many times they don't know how. So many people helped me in so many ways. Peter, a neighbor boy, mowed my lawn. Gerda cleaned my house. Dan ran endless errands. Dolly helped me sort out all of Larry's belongings. Many people listened and listened and listened some more.

It was a warm Friday evening in August when a nurse at the nursing home called to say that Larry had climbed over the railings and had fallen out of bed. They wanted me to go over and sign papers stating that I was aware of the fall and to give permission for any treatment that may be necessary. I hurried over, and on my way to the nursing station I peeked in at Larry. He was in bed, snuggling his teddy bear and whimpering. After signing the paper I passed his room again.

"Please," he cried, "come and read to me."

I told him I couldn't. I wasn't supposed to be in his room alone with him.

"Pleeeease," he begged. "I'm scared, and I need you."

In the book of Ecclesiastes, King Solomon wrote: "There is a time for every purpose under heaven." Determine that right now is the time you will

- *accept what God gives you.* "Give thanks in all circumstances, for this is God's will for you in Christ Jesus" (1 Thessalonians 5:18).

- *be content.* "For the Lord God is a sun and shield; the Lord bestows favor and honor; no good thing does he withhold from those who walk blameless" (Psalm 84:11).

- *hold earthly things with a light hand.* "I know what it is to be in need, and I know what it is to have plenty. I have learned the secret of being content in any and every situation" (Philippians 4:12).

- *accept what he allows into your life.* "Three times I pleaded with the Lord to take it away from me. But he said to me, 'My grace is sufficient for you, for my power is made perfect in weakness' " (2 Corinthians 12:8-9).

- *look toward your heavenly home.* "Do not let your hearts be troubled. Trust in God; trust also in me. In my Father's house are many rooms; if it were not so, I would have told you. I am going there to prepare a place for you. And if I go and prepare a place for you, I will come back and take you to be with me that you also may be where I am" (John 14:1-3).

How could I say no? After all, he was lying quietly in bed. So I went in, sat in the chair by his bed and started to read. Immediately he quieted down. Then suddenly, before I knew what was happening, he struck out with his foot and kicked my chair over backward. The back of my head struck the table behind me, and I sat on the floor stunned.

"Why did you do that?" I asked.

With an odd grin that had become hauntingly familiar Larry answered,

"Because I wanted to."

That was the last time I saw Larry alive. I got a call from the nursing home at 2:30 in the morning asking me to come right over. Larry had died peacefully in his sleep.

Larry's death was extremely traumatic for me, both physically and emotionally. Two days later I was hospitalized for complications of surgery I'd had a month before. I checked myself out of the hospital against doctors' orders to attend his memorial service.

Larry was gone. Nothing would ever be the same again.

But I would survive. I was God's child. And in his time I would be victorious.

16

Surviving Means
to Go On Living

AFTER LARRY DIED, I WAS BEYOND EXHAUSTION. "LET'S GO AWAY," I TOLD GERDA. "I want to go someplace where I can do nothing but sleep and think and pray."

After so many years of caring and giving care, death ushers in a tremendous period of adjustment. For so long my identity had been defined by Larry's physical and emotional needs. He dominated all my conversations, all my thoughts, my entire life schedule. When he was gone, I had to step back and figure out who I was.

I said goodbye to what was familiar to me. Now it was time to say hello to a forgotten way of life.

That Old Guilt
Should I have done something differently? Should I have done more? Did I have a right to go on living when Larry couldn't?

These questions plagued me all day and haunted my dreams at night.

Should I have done something differently?

Almost certainly.

Should I have done more?

Probably so.

Did I have a right to go on living when Larry couldn't?

What was my choice?

Whether you go away, as I did, or stay at home, it's time to consciously and systematically begin to pick up the pieces. Start by

- getting plenty of rest. (You know you are tired, but you're probably a lot more weary than you realize.)
- going to the doctor and getting a physical. (Your body has taken an incredible beating.)
- treating yourself well. (Indulge yourself. You've done enough sacrificing.)
- eating right. (Have balanced meals. Set the table and sit down to eat. No more standing at the sink.)
- getting enough exercise. (Even a walk around the block will get you started.)
- accepting challenges. (Surround yourself with encouraging people. Join a support group or get counseling if it would help. Learn to do something new. Plan some activities to get you out of the house.)
- getting outside of yourself. (Write letters. Watch children play. Do something thoughtful for someone else.)

Guilt comes with the territory. But you did what you did, and it was the best you could do at the time. The past cannot be retrieved. If you need to ask forgiveness for something done or left undone, do so. And at the same time, be ready to forgive those you believe were insensitive and thoughtless to you.

Yes, guilt is normal. But it is vital that you reconcile that guilt, or it will cause you harm, both physically and emotionally.

But there are warnings too.

- You may begin to feel amazingly energetic and euphoric, but proceed carefully. Your judgment may not be as acute and sharp as you think it is.
- Give yourself at least a year to regain your emotional balance.
- Don't make any big decisions (such as selling your house).
- Don't make major changes (such as getting remarried).

Your Spiritual Health

It is not uncommon to come through such soul-draining experiences as caregiving and death with a sense of spiritual weariness. You have prayed your hardest and trusted as thoroughly as you possibly could, yet the answer you received was not what you wanted.

So, what is the state of your spiritual health? Use this ten-point questionnaire to give yourself a spiritual check-up.

1. Love. Are you willing to invest your time and concern in others? What specifically are you doing to make such an investment?

2. Intimacy. Are you willing to reach out and share your experiences and what you have learned from them? Are you willing to risk giving support to someone else who needs it? Do you have at least one Christian friend with whom you are willing to share intimately?

3. Trust. Are you willing to be vulnerable rather than cautious, suspicious or cynical? In what ways do you allow yourself this vulnerability? With whom?

4. Meaning. Do you have a clear sense of God being in control of your life? Do you have a sense of being headed in a specific direction? Where?

5. Hope. Do you see yourself as having a future? What is it?

6. Faith. Do you believe God is working everything out for the best in your life even though things have not transpired the way you hoped? When you pray, are you willing to say, "Your will be done"?

7. Patience. Are you able to wait patiently and expectantly for God to work in his own time? Are you able to resist the temptation to push things along toward the resolution you believe is best?

8. Joy. Even in the darkest night and the most discouraging of circumstances, even when you are not at all happy, do you have a sense of joy? Does it fill what would otherwise be an empty shell of despair? Are you willing to let that joy bubble out and be seen by others?

9. Courage. Are you willing to face your limitations and to soar in spite of them? Do you firmly believe that through Christ all things are possible? When did you last stretch your limits?

10. Gratitude. Are you thankful to God for the life and circumstances he has allowed you? Do you truly appreciate the people who have walked alongside you and helped in ways big and small? For what are you thankful? How do you show your gratitude?

Changing Your Perspective

"Why, Lord, why?"

I have never yet met a caregiver who has not asked this question—usually again and again and again. I know I did.

We want answers. We want reasons. Sometimes, however, God doesn't give us any. And you know what? He doesn't have to. He is under no obligation to explain his purposes to us. God, in his mercy, may allow us to see good results from the tragedies in our lives, but then again he may not.

We can only see the immediate, but God sees eternity. Living a life of faith means being willing to trust our loving Father enough to turn all our questions over to him. It means releasing our demands to understand the reasons why.

Living by faith means readjusting our perspective from the immediate to the eternal. How can we do that? By reaching out to other people rather than inward to ourselves. By being committed to furthering God's kingdom rather than to satisfying our own narrow self-interests. By turning our eyes on Jesus rather than allowing ourselves to become obsessed with our own pain, grief and loss.

Right now your life may seem like the scattered pieces of a jigsaw puzzle. That's all right. But take comfort in knowing that God has his hands on the pieces. Already he is beginning to rearrange them and put them together to form a beautiful new picture.

Ask him to do it from his eternal perspective.

More Than Surviving
In the support group I attended, people talked about "surviving." I beg to differ. This is about more than surviving. It is about emerging victorious to a life that is richer and more abundant than it ever could have been had you not been a caregiver.

Six months after Larry died, I got a call from Donald who led the Sunday services at the nursing home where Larry had been. I hadn't been there since his death. In fact, I avoided that entire area of town. Donald said he was going to be away the following Sunday, and he wanted me to lead the service. "If you don't come, we will have to cancel," he said. "And you know how people here look forward to it."

I did know. But I also knew I didn't want to go. It was still too painful. Yet I reluctantly agreed.

The Sunday was beautiful and sunny, and all the roses in front of the nursing home were in full bloom. I lifted my head high and drank in the heady fragrance, then I walked resolutely through the front door.

The service went well. Les and Dorothy were at the organ and piano, and we sang the good old gospel hymns—we sang "The Old Rugged Cross" twice. Mimi sang her solo. Earlene asked questions. And I really was pleased to greet and hug my old friends. Kathleen asked me where I had been keeping myself. Gary smiled and squeezed my hand. Mary didn't recognize me, but she smiled anyway. Lyle asked me if I brought him anything.

I had walked out of the building and halfway across the parking lot when I stopped. I hadn't gone by Larry's old room. Maybe it would be good for me to do that. So I went back inside, down the hall to room 332, and peeked inside.

"Hello!" said a woman sitting by the bed. I recognized her from the service. "Did you come to visit with my husband?" she asked excitedly.

I looked at the withered man lying in Larry's bed, looking blankly up at me.

"This is my husband, Wes," the woman said. "He just moved in here. You are the first person to come and visit him."

I sat down, and she and I talked for awhile. I told her it was my husband's old room. She cried as she confessed to her own feelings of guilt and frustration and fear. I cried as I told her I knew just how she felt. Then we held hands and prayed together. Before I left, I read Psalm 23 to her husband. Larry used to like that.

I could see that woman was going to emerge victorious.

A New Beginning

The only true security any of us has comes from God, through the unconditional love found in a personal relationship with Jesus Christ. And Christ himself promises to meet our needs. In his letter to the Christians at Philippi the apostle Paul wrote: "He who began a good work in you will carry it on to completion until the day of Christ Jesus" (Philippians 1:6).

Our God is a God of new beginnings.

He is a God of hope and joy.

Let us join with David the psalmist and sing:

Weeping may remain for a night,
but rejoicing comes in the morning. (Psalm 30:5)

Appendix 1

Nursing Home
Checklist

Name of Facility: _____

Look at the residents and the staff.

☐ Do the residents seem relatively content?

☐ Is the staff friendly and courteous?

☐ Are the residents clean, combed and dressed appropriately for the temperature?

☐ Are they involved in a variety of activities?

☐ Are the activities tailored to the residents' individual needs and interests?

☐ Is the food nutritious and attractively served?

☐ Are an individual's personal food likes and dislikes taken into account?

☐ Does the home use care in selecting roommates?

☐ Is there a resident's council? If so, does it influence decisions about resident life?

☐ Is there a family council? If so, does it influence decisions about resident life?

☐ Are the administrator and staff available to discuss problems?

☐ Do volunteers from the community work with the patients?

☐ Do various staff members and professionals participate in evaluating each resident's needs?

☐ Does the resident or his family participate in developing a plan for his care?

☐ Does the home offer such programs as physical therapy, occupational therapy and speech therapy?

☐ Does the nursing home have an arrangement with a nearby hospital?

☐ Are specialists in various therapies available when needed (such as a dentist or podiatrist)?

☐ Are barbers and beauticians available?

Look at the facility itself.

☐ Is the home clean and in good repair?

☐ Is it cheerful?

☐ Is it well lighted?

☐ Are outdoor areas accessible for residents and their families to use?

☐ Are those areas attractive?

☐ Are there handrails in the hallways and grab bars in the bathrooms?

☐ Can residents in wheelchairs easily move around the home?

☐ Are the hallways large enough for two wheelchairs to pass each other safely?

☐ What equipment is there in the activity rooms (games, books, piano)?

☐ What physical therapy equipment is available?

☐ Are there nurse call bells in all the bathrooms?

☐ Does the noise level fit the activities that are going on?

☐ Are residents' rooms furnished pleasantly and with personal touches?

☐ Does each room have a window?

☐ Is there easy access to each bed?

☐ Is there at least one comfortable chair for each patient?

☐ Does each resident have a closet and drawers for personal belongings?

☐ Is there space in the room for a wheelchair to maneuver?

Appendix 2

List of Resources

This resource list cannot begin to include all that is available to you. Some of the best resources are local ones. Look in your telephone book. Check your newspaper. (The one I subscribe to has an entire page of resources that covers everything imaginable—and some things that aren't!) And ask. Ask other caregivers, and ask every professional you encounter.

If you have access to the Internet, use it for research. You will find a great deal of information, including local Web sites and support groups.

Specific Conditions
AIDS Information Hotline
(800) 342-2437

Alzheimer's Association
National Headquarters
919 North Michigan Avenue, Suite 1000
Chicago, IL 60611-1676
(800) 272-3900
(312) 335-8700
<http://www.alz.org>

American Cancer Society
777 Third Avenue
New York, NY 10017
(212) 371-2900

American Foundation for the Blind, Inc.
15 West 16th Street
New York, NY 10011
(212) 620-2000

American Heart Association
7320 Greenville Avenue
Dallas, TX 75231
(214) 750-5300

American Lung Association
1740 Broadway
New York, NY 10019
(212) 245-8000

The American Parkinson Disease Association
1250 Hylan Boulevard, Suite 4B
Staten Island, NY 10305-1946
(718) 981-8001
(800) 223-2732

Arthritis Foundation
1314 Spring Street NW
Altanta, GA 30309
(404) 872-7100

Cancer Information Service Hotline
(800) 4 CANCER

National Paraplegia Foundation
333 North Michigan Avenue
Chicago, IL 60601

National Spinal Cord Injury Foundation
369 Elliot Street
Newton Upper Falls, MA 02164

Stroke Club International
805 12th Street
Galveston, TX 77550
(403) 762-1022

Dealing with the Aged
American Association of Retired Persons (AARP)
National Headquarters
1909 K Street NW
Washington, D.C. 20049
<http://www.aarp.org/caregive>
Post questions and comments at the Caregivers Circle at <http://www.aarp.org/healthguide>

Children of Aging Parents
2761 Trenton Road
Levittown, PA 19056
(215) 945-19056

Family Caregiving Options
<http://www.aoa.dhhs.gov/aoa/webres/family.htm>
This online site offers directories for caring for the aged by the Department of Health and Human Services.

The National Association of Professional Geriatric Care Managers
1604 North Country Club Road
Tucson, AZ 85716

National Council on the Aging
600 Maryland Avenue SW
West Wing 100
Washington, D.C. 20024
Write to ask for a free listing of publications on the aging.

National Support Center for Families of Aging
P.O. Box 245
Swarthmore, PA 19081
(215) 544-5933
Among other things, this organization publishes "Help for the Families of Aging."

Senior Citizens Centers
These are available across the country. Listings are available through the National Council on the Aging (see address above).

United States Administration on Aging Web site
<http//www.aoa.gov>
This site gives details on local resources and links to other useful Web sites.

General Information
A Checklist of Concerns/Resources for Caregivers (Booklet # D12895)

A Path for Caregivers (Booklet #D12957)

These publications are free and can be obtained from
American Association of Retired Persons
AARP Fulfillment EE0684
601 E Street, NW
Washington, D.C. 20049

Caregiver Assistance Network
<http://www.cssdoorway.org/>
This online site sponsored by the Catholic Church provides links to a variety of
caregiver resources.

Caregiving Online: Wellness for Caregivers of an Aging Relative, Friend or Neighbor
<http://www.caregiving.com>
There is a great deal of valuable information for caregivers available on the "Online
Support" section of this homepage. A section called "Links for Caregivers" pulls
together sites that offer information on maintaining caregiver health.

Caregiver Survival Resources
<http://www.caregiver911.com>
This site presents a comprehensive list of quality caregiving links on the Internet.

Concerned Relatives of Nursing Home Patients
P.O. Box 18820
Cleveland Heights, OH 44118
(216) 321-0403
This organization provides many resources, including education, information and
support in all areas involving nursing-home residents and their care, including
social services, insurance and legislative acts.

Eldercare Locator
(800) 677-1116
<http://www.aoa.dhhs.gov/elderpage/locator.html>
This nationwide database gives caregivers lists of local resources providing services to the elderly, including support groups for caregivers.

Family Caregiver Alliance
425 Bush Street, Suite 500
San Francisco, CA 94108
(415) 434-3388
In California, (800) 445-8106
<http://www.caregiver.org/>
E-mail questions can be sent to <info@caregiver.org>.
This nonprofit organization assists family caregivers of adults suffering from brain impairments. It focuses on long-term care in the home and charges no fee for consultations and advocacy. It provides short-term counseling on a sliding scale. For a low fee, they also provide a caregiver workshop. Its homepage has much useful material for any caregiver, including individual fact sheets that are also available by mail for a nominal fee.

Financial Aid for the Disabled and Their Families
Gail Ann Schlachter and R. David Weber
Reference Service Press
10 Twin Dolphin Drive, Suite B-308
Redwood City, CA 94065
This organization gives information on grant funding and loans available to help disabled persons further their education.

Interim Health Care
(800) 641-0444
This is one of the nation's largest home health care providers. Their nurses, therapists, home health aides, companions and other professionals can help people who would otherwise have to be institutionalized to be able to stay at home.

JAF Ministries (Joni and Friends)
P. O. Box 3333
Agoura Hills, CA 91301
(818) 707-5664
<http://www.jafministries.com>
Newsletter e-mail <jafnews@jafministries.com>

National Family Caregivers Association
9621 East Bexhill Drive
Kensington, MD 20895-3104
(800) 896-3650
(310) 942-6430
<http://www.nfcacares.org>
This national not-for-profit membership organization provides members with services and products including a twelve-page newsletter. Dues are $20/year.

National Hospice Organization
1901 North Fort Meyer Drive, Suite 902
Arlington, VA 22209
(703) 243-5900

National Organization on Disability
910 16th Street, NW, Suite 600
Washington, D.C. 20006
(800) 695-0285

Ombudsman Program
(800) 231-4024
The Ombudsman Program is a resource for patients or residents of nursing homes. Call for a referral to the Ombudsman Program in your county.

Social Security Administration
(800) 772-1213
Call them for information on Medicare and Social Security eligibility.

Well Spouse Foundation
P. O. Box 58022
Philadelphia, PA 15909
This group can steer you to a support group in your area. If there isn't one, they can assist you in getting one started. They also put out an extremely helpful newsletter.

Appendix 3

Further Reading

One of the best things you can do for your loved one and for yourself is to read. Read all you can on the disability from which your loved one is suffering. Read the inspirational stories of others who have walked this road and have come through it. Read devotions and meditations that will lighten and uplift your soul. Whatever your loved one's physical situation, you will find books here that will help you and will help you help him or her.

Alzheimer's Disease

Fish, Sharon. *Alzheimer's: Caring for Your Loved One, Caring for Yourself.* Carol Stream, Ill.: Harold Shaw, 1990.

Gray-Davidson, Frena. *Alzheimer's Disease Frequently Asked Questions: Making Sense of the Journey.* Los Angeles: Lowell House, 1999.

————. *The Alzheimer's Sourcebook for Caregivers: A Practical Guide for Getting Through the Day.* Los Angeles: Lowell House, 1996.

Hodgson, Harriet. *The Alzheimer's Caregiver: Dealing with the Realities of Dementia.* New York: John Wiley and Sons, 1997.

Mace, Nancy, and Peter V. Rabins, M.D. *36-Hour Day: A Family Guide to Caring for Persons with A.D., Related Illnesses, and Memory Loss Later in Life.* New York: Warner Brothers, 1992. (This book can be obtained through the national headquarters of Alzheimer's Disease and Related Diseases Association, 70 Lake Street, Chicago, IL 60601-5997.)

Aging and Dealing with the Aged

Cohen, Donna, and Carl Eisdorfer. *Caring for Your Aging Parents: A Planning and Action Guide.* New York: Tarcher/Putnam, 1995.

Loverde, Joy. *The Complete Eldercare Planner: Where to Start, Questions to Ask, And How to Find Help.* New York: Hyperion, 1997.

McKenna, David L. *When Our Parents Need Us Most: Loving Care in the Aging Years.* Carol Stream, Ill.: Harold Shaw, 1994.

National Council on Aging. *Channels of Communications for Reaching Older Americans.* Washington, D.C., 1985.

Pritikin, Enid, and Trudy Reece. *Parentcare Survival Guide: Helping Your Folks Though the Not-So-Golden Years.* New York: Barron's Educational Series, 1993.

Walker, Susan C. *Keeping Active: A Caregiver's Guide to Activities with the Elderly.* San Luis Obispo, Calif.: American Source Books, 1994.

Books by Joni

Tada, Joni Eareckson. *Diamonds in the Dust: 366 Sparkling Devotions.* Grand Rapids, Mich.: Zondervan, 1993.

————. *Heaven: Your Real Home.* Grand Rapids, Mich.: Zondervan, 1997.

————. *The Life and Death Dilemma: Suicide, Euthanasia, Suffering, Mercy.* Grand Rapids, Mich.: Zondervan, 1997.

Tada, Joni Eareckson, with Steve Estes. *When God Weeps: Why Our Suffering Matters to the Almighty.* Grand Rapids, Mich.: Zondervan, 1997.

All of these are available from

JAF Ministries

The Disability Outreach of Joni Eareckson Tada

P. O. Box 3333

Agoura Hills, California 91301

(818) 707-5664

General Helps (Books)

Carter, Rosalynn. *Helping Yourself Help Others: A Book for Caregivers.* New York: Random House, 1996.

Larson, Elsie J., Deborah Hedstrom, Marcia A Mitchell and Lucibell Van Atta. *Strength for the Journey: Daily Encouragement for Caregivers.* Carol Stream, Ill.: Harold Shaw, 1999.

Meyer, Marcia M., and Paula Derr. *The Comfort of Home: An Illustrated Step-by-Step Guide for Caregivers.* Portland: CareTrust, 1998.

Schonhoff, Shelly, and Joanna Speaker. *Family Caregiver Guide: A Comprehensive Handbook for Caring for Your Loved One at Home.* Dubuque, Iowa: Simon & Kolz, 1998.

Strong, Maggie. *Mainstay.* Chester, N.J.: Bradford Books, 1997.

Tepper, Lynn M., and John A. Toner. *Respite Care Programs.* Philadelphia: Charles Press, 1993.

General Helps (Publications and Addresses)
How to Get Care from a Board and Care Home (1994)
Prepared by attorneys of the Nursing Home Advocacy Project
Bet Tzedek Legal Services
145 South Fairfax Avenue, Suite 200
Los Angeles, CA 90036

Medicare Made Easy (1999)
Charles B. Inlander and Charles MacKay
People's Medical Society
462 Walnut Street
Allentown, PA 18102
This is a clear, practical guide to the confusing world of Medicare. It outlines steps for negotiating with physicians, filing claims and evaluating supplemental insurance coverage.

Nursing Home Companion (1997)
Prepared by Attorneys of the Nursing Home Advocacy Project
Bet Tzedek Legal Services
145 South Fairfax Avenue, Suite 200
Los Angeles, CA 90036

The Nursing Home Handbook
Caregiving
Essential Guide to Wills, Estates, Trusts and Death Taxes
These books, all put out by AARP, are available from
AARP Books
Scott, Foresman and Company
1865 Miner Street
Des Plaines, IL 60016

Inspirational Reading
Hayden, Edward V. *Beloved Sufferer.* Boston: Standard Publishing, 1987.
Kuebelbeck, Julie, and Victoria O'Conner. *Caregiver Therapy.* St. Meinrad, Ind: Abbey Press, 1995.
Lewis, C. S. *A Grief Observed.* Greenwich, Conn.: Seabury Press, 1963.
Miller, James E. *Autumn Wisdom: Finding Meaning in Life's Later Years.* Minneapolis: Augsburg, 1995.

———. *The Caregiver's Book: Caring for Another, Caring for Yourself.* Minneapolis: Augsburg, 1996.

Morgan, Richard L. *Autumn Wisdom: A Book of Readings.* Nashville: Upper Room Books, 1995.

Appendix 4

Encouragement
from the Source

Although there are many helpful resources available, there is only one ultimate source—God's holy Word. Listed here are but a few of the avenues and scriptural passages that can help you when your soul is crying out for comfort, understanding and direction.

Scripture on Tape
"The Living Testament" for *The Living Bible*
Tyndale House Publishers
Wheaton, IL 60187

Reigner Recording Library
Union Theological Seminary
Richmond, VA 23227
They have a large selection of religious tapes available. Ask for a catalog.

When You Need Comfort
☐ Psalm 18:2
☐ Psalm 18:30
☐ Psalm 23
☐ Psalm 27:1
☐ Psalm 61:1-3
☐ Isaiah 25:8
☐ John 14:27
☐ Romans 8:18
☐ Romans 8:35,37-39
☐ Romans 11:33-36
☐ 2 Corinthians 1:3-4

☐ 2 Corinthians 12:9
☐ Philippians 4:6-7
☐ 1 Peter 5:7

Read About Faith
☐ Genesis 15:1-6
☐ Psalm 119:65-72
☐ Proverbs 3:5-6
☐ Matthew 6:25-34
☐ Romans 3:21—5:11
☐ Hebrews 11

When You Need God's Direction
☐ Proverbs 2:1-6
☐ Romans 12:1-3
☐ Ephesians 5:15-20
☐ Colossians 1:9-14
☐ James 1:5-6

What the Bible Has to Say About Death
☐ Psalm 116:15-16
☐ John 12:23-26
☐ Romans 6:1-10
☐ 1 Corinthians 15:35-58

. . . And About Heaven
☐ Matthew 6:19—24
☐ Philippians 3:12—4:1
☐ Revelation 21